PRAISE FOR
THE FINANCIAL WELLNESS MANDATE

"This is a must-read business book. The six megatrends—demographics, the employer-employee relationship, behavioral economics, consumerism, the convergence of health care and financial care, and technology and big data—offer a framework for being the employer of choice for upcoming generations of workers. Daniel's book offers a visionary lead we can follow in attracting, hiring, and retaining the best of the best to any business."

> Pam Popp
> President, Retirement Services
> Lockton Companies

"*The Financial Wellness Mandate* captures the essence of being a business owner and the ability we have to empower our employees to be the best versions of themselves."

> Dr. Richard Chaifetz
> Founder, Chairman and CEO
> ComPsych Corporation

"*The Financial Wellness Mandate* is bursting with interesting ideas and practical takeaways. It is essential reading for any business that wants to hire top talent. Every business should own a copy."

> Brendan Mahoney
> Head of Insurance and Retirement Sales
> American Capital

"Well written, insightful, and inspiring! Daniel provides great anecdotes and advice for employers and their advisors navigating the complicated world of benefit plan design. Great read!"

> Barbara Delaney
> Founder and Principal
> StoneStreet Renaissance

"Looking into the future of work, Daniel reminds us that the financial fortunes of employer and employee have become permanently entwined. Employees need more help than ever in achieving financial wellness, and employers are perfectly positioned to offer that help. Read this book and the employer-employee code will be revealed.

Hugh O'Toole
CEO
Innovu

"Drawing from his roles as an investment banker, financial advisor, executive, public speaker, entrepreneur, teacher, and father, Daniel brings together conversations with thousands of employers and employees from microbusinesses to Fortune 500 companies. He encourages employers to think expansively about their benefits and the future financial wellness of their coworkers and offers the best formula for hiring and retaining talent."

Jim O'Shaughnessy
President
Sheridan Road Financial

"Easy to use and full of solid advice, from the foundations of financial wellness in the workplace to megatrends that will dominate the future. If you are part of the retirement and benefit ecosystem, this book should be your new go-to resource."

Charlie Nelson
CEO
Voya Retirement

"The elephant in the room is the massive amount of student loan debt in the U.S. As of 2020, it is roughly $1.7 trillion, and the average balance held by the class of 2018 alone is more than $29,000. *The Financial Wellness Mandate* leads the way for employers to address this problem and empower employees for life."

David Aronson
Founder and CEO
Peanut Butter

"If you're an HR or C-suite executive, then you need to read this book! Daniel does a masterful job of discussing the changing workplace and offers his own experiences, while challenging you to focus on the importance of addressing the financial wellness of your employees."

Ken Verzella
Former Head of Financial Wellness, Mass Mutual
Vice President, Participant Advisory Services at Empower Retirement

"The workforce of today demands much more than previous generations. *The Financial Wellness Mandate* is a must-read for anyone who wants to create a company that competes for talent. In an increasingly competitive business world, the lessons in this book are more important than ever."

Alison Cooke Mintzer
Publisher and Chief Investment Officer
PlanAdviser and PlanSponsor

"I love how Daniel integrates academic concepts that are easy to understand but powerful when implemented."

Hal Hershfield
Associate Professor of Marketing, Behavioral Decision Making,
and Psychology
UCLA Anderson School of Management

"The COVID-19 pandemic revealed to all of us the fragility of our financial, emotional, and physical well-being. Daniel has had a front-row seat and provides solutions that can help businesses and employees be more ready, more resilient, and better able to achieve a state of wellness."

Andrea Goodkin
Executive Vice President, Human Resources Consulting
HUB International

"The wellness journey Daniel takes us on in *The Financial Wellness Mandate* reflects our changing landscape. Life is not easy, and employers and employees need each other now more than ever to reach their destination."

Liz Davidson
Founder and CEO
Financial Finesse

"Daniel really understands the mindset and concerns of employees and the opportunity for employers."

Ami Hindia
Senior Vice President
Fidelity Institutional

"The more we can do to create better financial literacy early on, the better we can serve students, employees, and society as a whole."

Ian Connole
Head of Peak Performance
Dartmouth College

"Daniel understands what makes people and businesses tick and offers a hopeful view of financial wellness."

Jennifer DeLong
Managing Director, Head of Defined Contribution for the Americas
AllianceBernstein

"Millions of workers struggle with caregiving for loved ones. Daniel recognizes that corporate-sponsored wellness programs are the most elegant way to distribute solutions that offer them real relief."

Lindsay Jurist-Rosner
CEO, CoFounder
Wellthy

"*The Financial Wellness Mandate* will help you have better health, financial, and life outcomes!"

Kristine Knutson
CEO
How Impressive

"Outcomes, outcomes, outcomes. It's all about improving our business outcomes by improving employee outcomes. Daniel has been on the front lines of this concept since the beginning."

Ross Marino
Founder and CEO
Adviser2X

"Financial wellness will be a Millennial legacy and one that Daniel Bryant and his ideas will help us create."

Fred Barstein
Founder and CEO
The Retirement Advisor University (TRAU) and
The Plan Sponsor University (TPSU)

"A must-read for any HR manager, CEO, or decision-maker who helps your business compete for talent."

Katherine Lee
Vice President
HUB International

"The financial, physical, and emotional health of employers has never been so interdependent. Any sound benefits strategy must take this into account, and Daniel shows us how."

Jamie Greenleaf
General Partner
Cafaro Greenleaf
Founder and CEO
Tilt, Inc.

"Financial anxiety impacts all aspects of our lives. Daniel provides us with the road map to reduce individual stress and create more productive businesses."

Richard Tatum
President
Venwell Retirement

"AI and financial technology is driving the future of benefits, especially financial wellness. Daniel is a former baseball player, and with this book he has hit it out of the park."

Ross Zgnaver
Managing Director, Digital Wealth
Blackrock

"Daniel's book reminds us of the pressure up-and-coming workers are placing on employers to engage them with real financial wellness solutions. He reminds us that the challenge is great, but he also offers a refreshing optimism and concrete ways for executives to meet that challenge."

Joseph DeNoyior
National President, Retirement and Private Wealth
Hub International

"Daniel could not be more on target in his push for employers to align workplace benefits around total financial wellness. The more employers offer at each life stage and age in terms of relevant tools and advice, targeted communications, investment options, and custom plan design, the better off employees and businesses will be."

Will Coleman
Global Head of Retirement and Strategic Accounts
Franklin Templeton

The

FINANCIAL WELLNESS MANDATE™

Be the Employer of Choice by Offering the Benefits Today's Workers Want and Need Most

Daniel R. Bryant

ISBN 978-1-936961-02-3

Edited by Sharon Ben-Dov
Copyedited and proofed by Jody Amato
Illustrations/charts by LeAnne Poindexter
Cover and interior design by Paul Fitzgerald

Published by LINX

LINX, Corp.
Great Falls, VA 22066

www.linxcorp.com

Printed in the United States of America

Better outcomes for everyone!

Daniel

DEDICATION

To my parents, Rhys and Jayne Bryant, from whom I have learned everything, and to my daughters, Ainsley and Lily, both of whom I couldn't be more proud and I hope learn something from me. And to my brother, Tim, and sister Louise, who have always provided support and guidance in my life, and to God, to whom I owe everything.

ACKNOWLEDGEMENTS

There are so many people to thank. To my editor, Sharon, who helped fly the plane with a novice pilot and my editor, Jody, who helped land the plane. Steve Eunpu, my publisher, who was a steady hand with someone whose patience nestles at #9 on the list of The Eight Virtues.

To all of those from whom I have learned so much and helped inspire me to write the book: Jim O'Shaughnessy, my childhood friend from Mr. Newbury's fourth grade class, who improbably became my business partner and best friend; Betsy Sorensen, who provided enormous support throughout the entire process; and all of my colleagues at Sheridan Road and Hub International from whom I always learn something about myself, life, and business. A special shout out to employee #1 and the enormously talented Jeremy Weith.

Special thanks to:

- My YPO forum partners for always being there no matter what: Steve, Jim, Ravi, Adam, John, Tom, and Eric.

- My brothers and teammates and everyone (too many to mention) whom I can call a friend at my alma maters of Dartmouth College and Northwestern University.

- My Quarantined Patriots - Annie, Craig, Lorrie, Kristine, Andy, Mark and Missy - who reunited during the COVID pandemic to provide support and comic relief during these challenging times.

- Board donors and volunteers who enable the Sheridan Road Charitable Foundation to make such a difference in our communities.

- All of the various organizations and amazing humans I've had the privilege of meeting along the way—from the early organizers of the Chicago Street Project to the special community of the Chicago Club—who provide insights, connectivity, and a sense of purpose no matter where our travels or careers take us.

And to thought leaders Fred Barstein, Ross Marino, Brian Graff, Alison Mintzer, John Sullivan, Peter Dunne (Pete the Planner), Liz Davidson, and Dave Ramsey. Special mention to Fred, in whose class I developed the outline for the book; and to Ross Marino and the Excel and Outcomes conference teams that helped me synthesize my thoughts into this book.

There are literally hundreds of people that I have to thank for this book. However, I would like to recognize the following for engaging in long conversations around the notion of convergence across health, wealth, and emotional well-being, and the emergence of financial wellness as not just a topic, but our foundational future: Vishal Jain, Hugh O'Toole, Dan Houston, Ed Murphy, Charlie Nelson, Ami Hindia, Pam Popp, Art Laffer, Jeff Faber, Dr. Richard Chaifetz, Jeff Stevens, Jamie Greenleaf, Bill Yoerger, Jake Konaxis, David Aronson, Ken Verzella, Jenn DeLong, Hal Hershfeld, Charlie Wheelan, Punam Keller, Adam Durrett, Tom Kelly, Andrea Goodkin, Greg Poplarski, Will Coleman, Jessica Fox, Ned McNally, Tyler Neenan, Dan Ariely, Chris Sleggs, Randy Long, Fielding Miller, Ryan Schutty, Michael Domingos, Robert Kapito, Dominique Jordan Turner, Ernie Lopez, Dave Waters, Greg Schneider, Kristen Berman, Dean Karlan, Jamie Bentley, Brendan Mahoney, Roger Paradisio, Adam Durrett, Lindsay Jurist-Rosner, Barbara Delaney, Ian Connole, Katherine Lee, Dave Sherlock, Gary Kleinschmidt, Richard Darien, Richard Tatum, Rebecca Hourihan, Joseph Adams and Eric Milano.

We also had hundreds of clients who responded to surveys and provided feedback on what was working and not working within their companies, while bearing their own fears and anxieties as they navigated the complexities of the 2020 pandemic.

I also tip my hat to so many venture capitalists, private equity professionals, technologists, attorneys, and investors who shy away from the spotlight and never receive full public recognition, but whose feedback has been and remains invaluable to me. I will recognize all of you privately.

Thank-you to everyone I worked with within Sam Zell's organization, many of whom I still call close friends to this day; to those at Donaldson Lufkin & Jenrette (which I still consider the best investment bank of the 90s), and all the extraordinarily gifted technology minds that came through Robertson Stephens and are now running some of the most amazing organizations in the world.

I have included a list of all of the organizations and businesses with whom I have worked, where I unabashedly learned from and gained great understanding. And a big thank-you to all who participated in the development of this book from the following companies:

AIG	First Eagle
Alliance Bernstein/AB Global	Fidelity
Allianz	Franklin Templeton
American Beacon	Goldman Sachs
American Century	Great West
American Funds/Capital Group	Invesco
Ascensus	Ivy Investments
Aspire	John Hancock
Blackrock	JP Morgan Asset Management/
BNY Mellon	Retirement
Cohen & Steers	Lazard Asset Management
Columbia Threadneedle	Legg Mason
Cuna Mutual	Lincoln Financial
Empower Retirement	Lord Abbett

Mass Mutual

MFS

Nationwide

Natixis

Neuberger Berman

New York Life/Mainstay

Nuveen

One Ameirca/AUL

Pentegra

PIMCO

Principal

Prudential

Putnam

T. Rowe Price

TransAmerica

Securian

The Standard

State Street Global Advisors

Vanguard

Vestwell

Victory Capital

Virtus Investments

Voya

Table of Contents

FOREWORD

*By Vishal Jain, Head of Financial Wellness
Strategy and Development
Prudential Financial, Inc.*

The growing national focus by employers on workplace financial wellness programs is very encouraging—and, arguably, long overdue. These initiatives, which look beyond just retirement planning to help employees in a much broader way, are one of the best, most proven ways to improve financial health across American society—and for your employees.

Why are they so effective?

As a longtime executive in the financial services industry, I've come to believe employers play a pivotal role in improving employee financial wellness for several reasons:

- Workplace financial wellness programs are impactful because younger generations of workers especially—namely Millennials—trust their employers and increasingly look to them for help on financial matters.

- Many individuals' financial lives are centered at the worksite through retirement, health care, and other protection benefits that they access at work.

- The reach of employers makes them the perfect mass channel for reaching millions of employees—and consumers—quickly and consistently.

- Workplace financial wellness programs can drive lasting behavior change by engaging employees through a wide range of channels and offering relevant solutions at life's milestone moments, such as starting a family, buying a home, divorce, or retirement.

While those of us in the financial industry have long been concerned about the increasingly widespread economic fragility and lack of financial literacy among younger workers, a huge and sudden external shock in the form of the 2020 COVID-19 pandemic revealed the true and undeniable financial vulnerability of American families.

Just a few months after the pandemic began, Prudential's 2020 Financial Wellness Census found that the crisis had already negatively impacted at least half of Americans' finances. Fielded in May 2020, the study showed nearly one in five consumers' household income was cut by half following the pandemic's outbreak, with 17 percent losing employer contributions to a retirement plan, 14 percent losing health insurance, and 10 percent losing group life insurance benefits, eliminating critical safety nets. These small but stunning slivers of data reflect the broad impact of the pandemic.

While the pandemic was an outlier of an event, a moment in time, it revealed in the starkest possible way a foundational problem affecting the American workforce: the shaky finances of many households, including limited emergency savings and high levels of debt, as well as structural financial risks such as the coupling of health insurance to employment.

Employers saw the raw impact of the pandemic on their employees, and on their own families and loved ones, as the pandemic blurred the lines between work and home and highlighted financial wellness and other challenges facing families. Many employers made emergency changes to their benefits plans (which has never really happened in modern history, outside the cycle of open enrollment). In a matter of weeks, the pandemic reminded us how critical workplace benefits are to our financial stability and peace of mind. It also shifted the dynamic between employer and employee from one based on a financial contract to more of a compassionate partnership.

Unlike any event in recent history, the pandemic also has driven employers nationwide to focus much more intently on financial wellness programs. Now, more than ever, employers (and employees) are awake to how much help employees need to manage through financial stressors and how important it is to minimize the very real drag on business productivity that naturally occurs when a workforce is under significant collective stress.

Daniel Bryant, the author of this book, is a pioneer in the workplace financial wellness movement. As the Founder and CEO of Sheridan Road Financial (consistently ranked as a top institutional investment consultant by *Barron's* and *The Wall Street Journal*), Daniel recognized several years ago that delivering state-of-the-art retirement plans with high-quality investment options was necessary, but not enough, to ensure participants achieved financial security. He saw that employees needed assistance in overcoming barriers—such as reducing debt or budgeting effectively—to be able to save adequately for retirement. They needed meaningful help, fast, and the employer was and remains in the best position to deliver that help.

In response to this widespread need, Daniel expanded his practice to help plan sponsors understand and address the broader financial wellness needs of their participants. Sheridan Road was one of the first firms to explicitly include financial wellness as a key pillar in its recommendations for plan sponsors. Daniel and his firm also went beyond their commercial activities on financial wellness to support financial education, literacy efforts, and socially responsible programs within the community and continue to do so through the Sheridan Road Charitable Foundation.

Most importantly, Daniel is an equally staunch advocate for both the employer *and* the employee. He believes that by shining a bright light on the financial plight of working Americans—by stripping away any remaining denial we may have about our need for greater financial literacy, acknowledging the powerful role of the employer, and by having authentic, compassionate conversations about what is and isn't working—we can all work together to create innovative, practical solutions that create mutual benefit for both employers and employees.

The Financial Wellness Mandate builds on Daniel's work over the last decade to provide a compelling road map for employers of all sizes, in any industry, to realize the full promise of workplace financial wellness programs. In fact, the "Sheridan Road Map" was not only the name of the company's first newsletter, but also their inaugural financial planning engagement strategy. Engagement is the fuel for any wellness strategy—helping individuals understand their challenges, as well as available solutions and best practices, and motivating them to act.

For any executive or manager with a stake in employee benefits, workplace productivity, culture, human capital, or profitability, this book is a must-read. It details how workplace financial programs can drive engagement by leveraging behavioral finance, data analytics, and the best practices of leading consumer companies to provide benefits that make real human impact and engage upcoming generations of workers.

Most importantly, *The Financial Wellness Mandate* affirms a healthier, more human, more empathetic, more mutual relationship between employers and employees, based on a forward-looking model in which investing in financial wellness pays off for everyone.

INTRODUCTION

We are witnessing a seismic shift in business as Millennials replace the retiring Boomer workforce. Everything you thought you knew about employees is about to become obsolete.

Businesses that plan and adapt to the way this new generation thinks and acts will be in the position to attract, hire, and retain the best talent.

Those that ignore these changes could see their businesses decline and possibly fail.

The pages of this book were written for the leaders who want to see their businesses thrive in the decade ahead and beyond.

In the post-Industrial era, the relationship between employer and employee has become part financial contract, part social contract. Employees provide time and expertise. In return, employers provide salary, benefits, a career path, and a mission and culture to which employees are willing to devote roughly a third of their waking lives.

But as society evolves, and as new and unpredictable—even radically destabilizing—events occur and market forces evolve, and as stark generational differences between workers reveal themselves, the relationship between employer and employee has begun to change faster than ever.

The financial fortunes and fitness of employer and employee have become entwined in an unprecedented and irreversible way

I'm a seasoned financial industry veteran. I'm also an optimistic cynic—or perhaps a cynical optimist—when it comes to people and money. I know people generally have the best intentions when it comes to managing their money. I also know how emotional, confused, shortsighted, and even reckless humans can be regarding money. This is true regardless of their title, IQ, material assets, career, or socioeconomic status.

I also understand how bad even the most brilliant humans and businesses can be at scenario planning. We can use all manner of tools and prompts to try to plan for what's next. But sometimes we simply can't imagine what we can't imagine. In short, we have good intentions, but most of us are just "OK" at planning for the future.

I also see that employers generally have good intentions. They want to attract the best talent and offer the best possible benefits they can, while keeping costs low and profitability high. And they've tried everything from gym discounts to coveted box seats to foosball tables to nap pods. But a new day is dawning, and these once-sparkling ideas no longer hold the currency they once did.

Start with the statistics: the shaky state of financial wellness in the U.S.

The state of financial health in the U.S. is precarious and worrisome even to a thick-skinned industry expert like me. One huge problem is that our school systems and our family units are greatly lacking when it comes to teaching financial literacy. Consider a few stunning factoids:

- Eighty percent of Americans have insufficient savings for an emergency.

- Roughly 30 percent of Americans have no savings whatsoever (https://www.bankrate.com/banking/savings/financial-security-june-2019/).

- Seventy-five percent of American employees experience some sort of financial anxiety on a daily basis.

- And just a few years ago, a staggering 56 percent of student loan borrowers said they'd take a punch in the face from boxing legend Mike Tyson if it meant they could get out from under their student loans.[1]

These trends and countless others have long been a concern to industry watchers and employers who see employees struggling to juggle work and personal finances.

But as an industry, we just aren't doing enough to offer meaningful help.

However, "black swan" events like 9/11, the Great Recession of 2008, and the 2020 COVID pandemic have brought a singular reality crashing to the forefront:

American workers desperately need help making better financial decisions.

Not only do they need help planning for retirement, but they also need help managing their debt burdens, as well as with countless other day-to-day obligations, before they can even begin to think about retirement.

I believe employers are perfectly positioned to offer that help. And employers that do offer that help are the ones that will win at attracting, hiring, and retaining top talent over time.

These moments (like a recession, a pandemic, or consumers' brief love affair with pet insurance) don't last forever. But they are acute reminders of how interconnected—and fragile—our physical, financial, and emotional wellness and our ability to perform at work are. They also remind us how quickly employees and businesses can be destabilized or destroyed by that one freight train we never saw coming. They force us to snap out of complacency and to think about lofty ideas like "financial wellness" in a whole new light.

Waking up to the mandate for financial wellness

More employers are tuning in to the profound impact of employees' financial stability on personal and business performance. This truth has long had the attention of human resources teams. But the whole C-suite is now taking note. To some degree, they've been forced to take note in the era of COVID. They see what furloughs, layoffs, pay cuts, and intense stress have done to their employees, and they're feeling more connectivity and empathy with employees than ever before.

As I talk with employers nationwide, I see a shift happening almost day by day. Many companies used to think that offering a 401(k) plan, a few lunch 'n' learns, or a Cheesecake-Factory-length menu of random voluntary benefits was enough. But all of us, myself included, are rethinking the meaning of stability, resiliency, and wellness in every aspect of our lives. I'm thrilled to see executives beyond just HR, such as CFOs and COOs, attending and actively engaging at more of my client meetings than ever before.

We're at last coming to view employees, their finances, their entire well-being, and organizational performance through the lens of holistic outcomes.

We're also fully admitting that employees simply can't bring the best versions of themselves to work if their financial houses are in disarray. And, frankly, recent events have shown even the most hardened executives that it's simply inhuman to expect employees to do so.

Granted, employers are making progress: 53 percent of U.S. companies offer financial wellness programs today compared to just 24 percent in 2015. But we need to evolve further and faster if we want a focused, high-performing workforce and if we employers want to remain a brand of choice with top talent. And it's important to note that the vast majority of companies that make up the middle and small markets do not have any program whatsoever.

Why this book, why now?

I've spent more than twenty years as an investment banker and financial advisor to individuals, companies, and employee benefit plan sponsors. I now see market and human forces converging in an unprecedented way. I see hardworking people struggling, and I see employers grappling with their next best move in terms of employee benefits.

So I decided it was time to bring this book to life.

The Millennial tidal wave: it's here, it's big, and it's changing the benefits landscape in a major way

Millennials, the first true digital natives, now make up the bulk of the workforce. While their predecessors have been prone to dismiss Millennials as job-hopping, group-thinking, coddled, entitled whiners, Millennials have been quietly maturing, building families, moving into management, influencing digital delivery of solutions in every aspect of life, and even influencing legislation—all while trying to figure out how the heck to pay for basic life expenses like housing and student loans. They can't even think about saving for retirement. They're a quirky and demanding lot. And they're a force of nature we can't ignore.

- Fifty-three percent of Millennials would rather lose their sense of smell than their technology.

- Seventy-three percent of Millennials expect their employers to help them create a financial road map.

- Twenty-five percent of their paycheck goes toward student loan debt.

They demand the most from employers and are struggling the most financially. For employers whose mission, vision, and sense of social responsibility aligns with theirs, Millennials are stunningly loyal. Employers who can understand their true needs and offer the right financial wellness benefits to this segment will be an employer brand of choice for this dominant segment of the workforce.

This book is drawn from my role as an investment banker, financial advisor, executive, public speaker, entrepreneur, teacher, and father. It brings together conversations with thousands of employers and employees from microbusinesses to Fortune 500 companies. It also reflects insight from industry luminaries, innovators, and disruptors I am honored to call colleagues and friends.

It's borne most of all from my desire to help individuals achieve financial freedom and to help employers succeed. I find it heartbreaking to hear stories over and over of well-meaning, smart people who are living with paralyzing financial stress but who lack the means, direction, and tools to get out of it. I want to be a partner to employers and employees, so that together we can figure out the wacky new normal we're in and create an even greater value exchange between the employer and employee.

I'm certainly not the first author to offer advice to employers and their advisors. But I admittedly may be the most rabidly enthusiastic on the topic. There are countless books on hiring and retention, plan design, or how to achieve social impact and CSR goals—just to name a few. But I do believe that none have brought together these megatrends into a unified view you can use to deliver best-in-class benefits with a solid ROI.

Some of what we'll examine in this book

The foundations of financial wellness. We'll look at what financial wellness really means, how the benefits landscape has evolved, and how we've come full circle to now see (for better or worse) the employer as the new spirit guide to wellness for employees.

The biggest obstacles standing between us and financial wellness. We'll examine the biggest financial challenges—and the biggest drain on our monthly cash flows that we American workers face, including student loan debt, credit card debt, housing expenses, and the extraordinary medical expenses that can rock any of our lives at any given time.

The megatrends that'll upend the benefits landscape in the next decade. We'll dive into six key trends, below, that executives across functions must understand now in order to become or remain an employer brand of choice. Those companies that take heed of these trends will be best positioned to attract, hire, and retain the workforce of the future.

- **The undeniable force of behavioral economics**—the conscious and unconscious human behaviors and impulses that drive how we handle financial risk, and how we can exploit or overcome them.

- **Shifting demographics**—the changing composition of the workforce, critical generational nuances, and the massive impact Millennials have on the benefits landscape.

- **The rise of consumerism**—what buyers in all their forms now want and how an on-demand, digital-first economy is affecting the delivery of benefits and wellness solutions.

- **The convergence of health care and financial care**—how these worlds are now inextricably linked and how integrated solutions can improve outcomes for employees and employers.

- **The rise of big data and technology**—how together these can help us understand employees, the cost of various offerings, and how together they can help employers take targeting, decision support, and delivery of benefits to unprecedented new heights and be ready for what's next.

- **The changing relationship between the employer and employee**—how the employers' expanded role in their employees' lives can shape individual and collective financial, physical, and emotional life outcomes.

My hope for you and your management team

If you're reading this book, you're likely an expert in your business function. (Or perhaps you're a Millennial searching for answers or the parent of a Millennial or even a Zoomer in search of a resource for yourself or your kids.) But you're clearly also open to new ideas. As you read this book, in addition to the questions I pose at the end of each chapter, I hope it prompts you and your teams to ask the really big questions, such as:

- *Are we thinking as broadly as possible about financial wellness?*

- *Are we guessing at what our employees need? Have we asked them what they need, and do they all need similar things?*

- *What financial wellness benefits are our peers offering that we aren't?*

- *Why are we doing what we do? What are the ideal outcomes for our business? For our employees?*

I also hope it helps you think more expansively about your benefits offering and how important financial wellness is as part of your broader human capital strategy. I've tried also to offer sufficient data to consider a tailored, segmented approach to benefits if you haven't done so before. (And I'll explain within these pages how data analytics and technology is making this more feasible than ever.)

Above all, I hope this serves as a clarion call for why financial wellness is the most important, most urgent workforce-related issue for you to tackle now. Let's take a closer look and figure this out together.

BEHAVIOR NUDGES

The driving force of behavioral economics

Behavioral economics, now a full-blown field in its own right, animates most of our financial decisions whether we know it or not. Even the most analytical, financially savvy among us are, to some degree, governed by these human weaknesses and tendencies that are studied in detail by behavioral economic experts. That's why I've devoted one of this book's beefiest chapters to the topic, and why sprinkled throughout this book you'll see what I find to be some of the most interesting and relevant aspects of behavioral economics when it comes to understanding the workforce and finding ways to empower them to improve their financial wellness.

PART I—FOUNDATIONS OF FINANCIAL WELLNESS IN THE WORKPLACE

The idea of "financial wellness" is one that has matured before our very eyes. It has grown from a narrow discussion to one that encompasses virtually every aspect of our personal and professional worlds and has a profound impact on our ability to live stable and fulfilling lives. Before we look to the future of financial wellness, it's critical that we look at its history and its current foundations and influences. Join me in examining one of the most important ideas of our time.

THE FINANCIAL WELLNESS MANDATE

"Without financial wellness, there is no overall health and wellness. Organizations that embrace this mantra by helping their employees with financial issues will themselves be healthier and wiser!"

—Dr. Richard Chaifetz, Neuropsychologist and philanthropist

Welcome to the new workplace

The one where the employer has become the guardian, guide, and enabler of total employee wellness. Career wellness. Physical wellness. Emotional wellness.

And now add to that *financial wellness.*

It's no longer a wish-list item for employers. There's a clear mandate. And it's begun to accelerate at light speed, driven by a number of factors.

How'd we get here? We'll get into that.

But first, a few facts to toss up on the whiteboard:

- Over 50 percent of the world's population is under thirty years old.

- The average attention span of an American is seven seconds. (Basically, only a hair better than a squirrel or a goldfish.)

- In 2020, only twenty-one states required that high-school students take some sort of financial literacy course work. [1]

- The biggest, most powerful segment of the workforce, Millennials, saw their parents and grandparents punched in the face by the Great Recession of 2008.

- More people on this planet own a mobile device than a toothbrush. Don't worry, I have no commentary on the merits of good dental hygiene. But it does beg the question . . .

- And, of course, the declining financial wellness of employees has been greatly aggravated by destabilizing events such as the 2020 COVID-19 pandemic.

It is within this context that "financial wellness" has become far more than just a corporate catchphrase.

It's now part of our everyday vernacular. Human Resources can't talk enough about it. Corporate boards are updating their mission statements to include references to financial wellness. Companies of all sizes and across all sectors are rolling out financial wellness strategies as a way to attract and retain new talent—especially Millennials. And venture capitalists and private equity firms are investing more money in the financial technology (fintech) that powers financial wellness tools at a pace that would have been unfathomable just five years ago.

This is all in response to the growing reality—and opportunity it presents—of financial distress among working Americans and the overwhelming gulf between financial stress and financial freedom.

And yet, as I travel the country talking to investors and employers alike, it's evident we still have a lot to learn about what financial wellness means, how it became so relevant so fast, why we all should collectively care, and what steps we need to take in order to actually help working Americans while still running profitable companies and remaining true to our business roles.

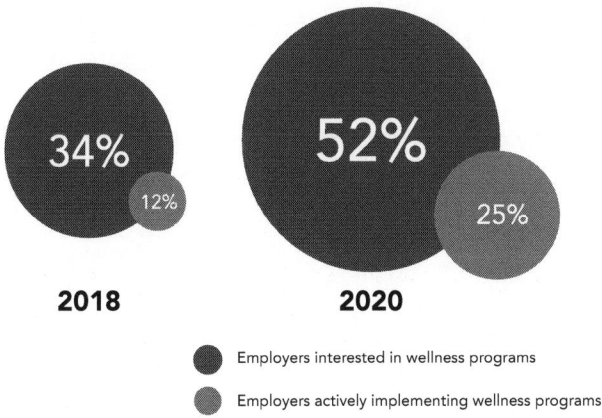

Employers are increasingly interested in offering wellness programs, but employee appetite is still outpacing their availability.

Source: https://www.ebri.org/docs/default-source/ebri-issue-brief/ebri_ib_515_fwes2020-22oct20.pdf?sfvrsn=34693a2f_4

First things first: we need a common definition of financial wellness

We all throw the term "financial wellness" around. But what does it *mean*? To some, it means a 401(k) program. To others, it means offering some lunch 'n' learns or webinars on investing. To others, it means tossing in a health savings account (HSA) or an à la carte benefit or two and calling it a "financial wellness" program.

Others define it based on what it is *not*. Phil Waldeck, President of Prudential, puts it this way: "I will tell you that if you had ten people in the room and asked them what financial wellness is, you'd have ten different answers. But I know one thing: I know what financial *illness* is. That is something people can define, and it hits home."

I couldn't agree more.

I often compare financial wellness to a life journey. It's that road along which we travel, moving from a state of financial stress or anxiety to one of financial freedom or independence. It's more like San Francisco's famously hilly and winding Lombard Street than a wide-open freeway. (Trust me, I've run Lombard many times. I know.) But there is a definite direction and end game, and it usually encompasses a broad array of tools, resources, technology, and planning to get there. We use all of these resources at our disposal so that we can achieve our ability to choose to start that version 2.0 of our lives. That entire journey of goal-oriented financial decision-making is financial wellness.

Alternatively, and more to the point, financial wellness can be defined as the following:

A state in which a person is able to adequately meet their daily financial obligations, can absorb short-term emergencies, feels empowered to plan and save for the future, utilizes debt strategically, amasses adequate resources to live a life of dignity in retirement, and is able to transcend mere survival to achieve peace of mind and personal fulfillment for themselves and their loved ones.

It's a lofty vision. But one I believe is achievable.

I've been thinking deeply on this topic for years. Since I first read *Nudge: Improving Decisions About Health, Wealth, and Happiness*, the groundbreaking 2009 book by Richard Thaler, I haven't been able to stop thinking about the ideas I'll share with you in this book. That book had a profound impact on me and cemented my view that employers and employees could work as partners to "nudge" big obstacles out of the way and use small shifts to create huge positive impacts in financial wellness.

For me, the third chapter of that book, titled "Save More Tomorrow," was absolutely crucial. (And that idea was then explored in a full book of the same name by UCLA Professor of Economics Shlomo Benartzi.)

But for me, saving more for tomorrow was only half the story. We have absolutely no hope of saving more for tomorrow if we don't BORROW LESS TODAY. Why? Because it just so happens that the top four obstacles standing between us and financial wellness relate in some way to debt. We borrow, borrow, borrow (and to make it worse, we're awful at distinguishing wants from needs, and most of us have never been taught how to use debt strategically rather than frivolously), and it leaves us stressed. Above all, it drains us of our ability to save for basic emergencies, much less save more for any sort of "tomorrow."

First, we need to look at the current state of financial anxiety and why so many American workers are so far from realizing even a semblance of financial wellness.

The quiet epidemic: financial stress in the workplace

More than 75 percent of Americans are living every single day with some sort of financial stress. It's like a big, black cloud that follows millions of American workers day and night. It causes inefficiencies, truancy, absenteeism, poor work productivity, marital issues, and family problems. It is also directly correlated to health issues. Financial stress is like a powerful but heartless motivator—pushing us forward each day but not necessarily adding to our true well-being or peace of mind.

"People can't invest in their long-term financial security when they are focused on making ends meet right now. We may face an uncertain reality during moments like the COVID pandemic or other unexpected events, but the savings crisis is one thing that will certainly continue without the collective action needed to innovate and scale solutions. This is the moment for employers, payroll providers, record keepers, and policymakers to come together and make short-term savings accessible to more and more people," explains Deborah Winshel, Global Head of Social Impact at Blackrock, which has been a leader in the effort to make cash savings vehicles more top of mind for employers and employees.

If we look back a little more than a decade, we can see that this problem has been building for a long time. During the Great Recession of 2008–2009, the increase in Google searches related to migraines, heart attack symptoms, ulcers, high blood pressure, and visits to urgent care facilities were up more than 200 percent.

It doesn't matter if you are twenty-two or sixty-two. Generationally or geographically, we're all living with some sort of financial anxiety.

One huge reason: we tend to excel at spending but not at understanding or managing money.

In fact, we're experts at spending money. And our kids are getting even better at it than we are. We have it down to an art. We will buy almost anything. Just ask Amazon and all the other data-driven companies that know how to tempt us with just the right impulse item at the moment of checkout and count on us getting those nice little dopamine rushes when we click "buy now" or when the next package lands on the front porch. Avocado slicer, anyone? Bouncy ball chair? Motorized standup desk? Why not?!

BEHAVIOR NUDGES

Hyperbolic Discounting

People tend to put an overly high value on the here and now and an overly low value on the future. This can lead to chronically poor decision-making when it comes to personal finance and our overall financial wellness.

It reminds me of a funny bit comedian Jerry Seinfeld does on "Nighttime Jerry" versus "Morning Jerry." Nighttime Jerry makes all kinds of bad decisions—from beer benders to binge-watching to big-ticket impulse buys—that Morning Jerry has to pay for the next day. It captures perfectly how easily we can distance ourselves from our own behavior . . . until we can't anymore. Leading behavioral economist and UCLA Associate Professor of Psychology, Marketing, and Behavioral Decision Making Hal Hershfield calls this the phenomenon of "the future self": one in which we have this rather bizarre inability to conceive how today's choices can come back to haunt us tomorrow. Our brains neurologically actually think of this future person in the third person. It has profound effects when thinking about harmful things we do to ourselves today that we think we in our present won't have to deal with, but rather that person in thirty years who happens to have the same name as me. Smoking is the classic example of this. We have this quirky and dangerous ability to distance our current selves from our future selves when that future self is us. It makes you wonder how early humans ever survived, or weather crises like periods of food scarcity and rationing, which demanded that we grow and store food for the coming winter without breaking into our stores today. We've been evolving for thousands of years, and we still haven't learned that we can't outrun our own shadows.

The tragic fact is, thanks to human quirks like these, we have an entire generation of Americans who are utterly ill-equipped to deal with current life expenses, much less retirement. The statistics are alarming.

- Roughly 80 percent have insufficient savings in case of an emergency.

- Upwards of 75 percent experience some sort of financial anxiety.

- Nearly 75 percent expect employers to be responsible for the financial well-being of employees.

- More than 70 percent struggle with paying monthly household expenses.

- Over 60 percent report that finances are the main source of stress in their lives.

- Just under 50 percent say their spending equals or exceeds their income.

- Approximately 45 percent do not have enough savings to cover living expenses for three months.

- More than 40 percent use credit to make ends meet.

- Over 40 percent have no retirement savings.

Want proof beyond the stats? Start pontificating about stocks, bonds, puts, calls, shorts, and CITs at your next PTO meeting or at the water cooler at work, and just see how fast the color drains from your friends' and colleagues' faces. That's the dread-and-utter-lack-of-confidence look. While financial wellness and money management should be one of the top three life skills, it ranks as number thirteen or even thirty for most of us. Roger Paradisio, Head of Technology for Franklin Templeton, laments, "It's virtually impossible for anyone to be able to plan or juggle the daily blitzkrieg of financial obligations coming at them every day without a single class or understanding of what is at stake. How can you play the game when you don't know what the rules are nor the consequences?"

Why the workplace is the right repair lab for financial wellness

There are myriad reasons employers are the most logical channel through which to provide financial education, guidance, tools, and the technology that can help us make meaningful advances in financial wellness. A few of them:

- Employers already provide retirement plans, health insurance, voluntary benefits, health savings accounts, and employee assistance programs (EAPs). And they own the payroll platforms off which all these other rapidly evolving services easily hang.

- Perhaps most importantly, the workplace is the primary point of decision-making for the individual. It is where individuals spend the bulk of their waking time.

- If a company's ethos, strategy, and inherent moral compass align in particular with its Millennial employee demographic, then that segment of employees will be deeply loyal, stay longer and, correspondingly, accept any advice, direction, or guidance provided by the employer. (We take a much closer look at this huge and forceful segment of the workforce and their behaviors in Chapter 6.)

The historic arc of employee benefits and financial wellness in the workplace

The underlying idea of financial wellness has certainly been a part of benefit planning for decades. To use my own company as an example, we were putting financial wellness slides in our Sheridan Road Financial overview books targeted to employers as early as 2005. Your company has probably been doing the same for years as well.

But it should also be noted that what we were referring to more than a decade and a half ago was not nearly as broad as the modern view of "financial wellness." Ours—like that of so many other employers at that time—was an early, rather narrowly defined version, focused on making everyone feel good, offering lunch 'n' learns on a few financial, investment, and savings topics. And while we never tracked this precisely, I'm pretty sure that even though my presentations were engaging and, at least in my eyes, extremely funny, there is no doubt the employees were there mostly for the free lunch and time away from their desks. Come to think of it, Chipotle or Pasta Day were always the bigger draws. Things that may make you go "hmmmm." The other, more serious and more human reality is that transparency and authenticity weren't as in vogue in society, frank discussions about money struggles were still implicitly taboo, and everyone sat around smiling and nodding as if their situation was entirely under control and they weren't secretly panicking inside.

And many of the Fortune 500 companies have been talking at some level about financial wellness since the 1990s. But for much of that time, we were really only talking about what I've described above: some sort of onsite financial education, maybe some lunch 'n' learns about investment options or a complimentary session with a financial advisor from your plan administrator or record keeper.

But it is widely viewed that the modern-day version of financial wellness— with a more acute definition, backed by technology and more substantive facts, and infinitely better positioning and marketing behind it—wasn't coming into view until 2015. At that time, financial wellness morphed from a throwaway comment at a conference to center-stage conversation.

In my conversations with some of the leading voices in the space—Vishal Jain, Head of Financial Wellness, Prudential (and author of this book's Foreword); Ken Verzella, Head of Financial Wellness, Empower and Mass Mutual; Charlie Nelson, Chief Executive Officer, VOYA Financial; and Peter Dunne (Pete the Planner)—there is strong general consensus that it was roughly 2015 when "financial wellness" went from being a sales tag line for a very limited offering to a real conversation with companies around how to improve individual and business outcomes by thinking more holistically about financial wellness. As a matter of fact, my friend Bill Yoerger, former President of One America/American United Life Insurance Company® (AUL), openly admits that, prior to 2015, financial wellness was used purely as a "shiny rock"—a somewhat hollow differentiator—used to try to help his company sound a bit unique compared to other record keepers. Bill recalls, "We had good intentions at the time and thought we were being pretty innovative in using the term 'financial wellness.' It wasn't until we hired Pete the Planner, as part of a marketing program, that we realized, "HOLY COW!," our people *really* need someone to talk to about their finances. We didn't know what we didn't know, and it was an important part of our own evolution in realizing just how powerful the idea of true financial wellness was."

The conversation had shifted. The time was right. Companies were ready to talk about it, fintech vendors and advisors were ready to push the envelope, employees were ready to accept it, and the technology was finally available to track and analyze it. This just happened to coincide with the rapidly changing demographics in this country with the maturing of Millennials, historically low unemployment, and a twelve-year bull market that had driven consumer debt to unprecedented levels. A combination of ballooning student loans, credit card and health-care debt, coupled with the lack of consumer finance understanding, had created the crucible needed for real financial wellness solutions to begin taking form.

In addition, it was at this time that the concept of total financial wellness (and the workplace as its epicenter) began to get legs. The industry outlets defining the space and watching (and leading) trends began adding certain tracks, panels, and keynote speakers to their conference agendas. Something was happening, and it was starting to feel like a bona fide movement.

By the way, one of most fun and gratifying parts of writing this book has been reaching out to numerous colleagues and fellow thought leaders in the benefits industry (and many of them longtime friends and experts I admire greatly) to get their take on the financial wellness movement. In talking with these longtime industry experts, it became clear that we all shared a strong sense that it was in late 2015 when financial wellness suddenly began to appear everywhere we turned. Clearly, its day was coming.

It's also interesting to look at the major industry conferences and their agendas not long after that, beginning in 2016. In 2016, health savings accounts (HSAs) were addressed by a small panel that Jamie Greenleaf, Managing Partner, Cafaro Greenleaf and CEO of Tilt, and I headlined. There were a whopping twenty people in the breakout room. By 2019, Rekon/Adviser2x (organizers of the EXCEL Conference) launched Outcomes, an entire conference dedicated to financial wellness, and Plan Sponsor was able to support an entire conference focused on HSAs alone, with myself and Jamie as the keynote speakers. If you had tried to tell me just a few years or even months earlier that the industry could have supported an entire conference on HSAs, I'm not sure I would have believed you.

This all signaled to me that financial wellness was an idea whose time had finally come.

Who's offering financial wellness programs now

While estimates and definitions vary, it's safe to say that well over half of employers now offer some sort of financial wellness program. And that number is growing by the day. For example, a 2019 survey from Bank of America showed that 53 percent of respondents were offering financial wellness programs, compared to just 24 percent in 2015. (While an impressive relative increase, it should be noted that there still exists a large chasm between the *Forbes* Global 2000—the magazine's annual ranking of the world's largest public companies—and the small- and middle-market companies in this country that employ a majority of Americans.)

While it took some time to take hold, financial wellness in the workplace is now an idea that seems to be skyrocketing. For more than two years, our team has been asked by employers about the topic on almost a daily basis. Even in 2014 (which in the digital era admittedly feels like forever ago), when the Consumer Financial Protection Bureau was then only three years old, the fledgling agency published a hefty forty-five-page report on "Financial Wellness at Work." The report's introduction reminds us that the workplace is where "people make some very important financial decisions." They also pointed at that time to the preliminary evidence showing that "a financially capable workforce is more satisfied, more engaged, and more productive for their employers." [2]

And as the report also rightly notes: "Workers don't leave their money worries at home."

Ideas like this remind us that we can gloss over the state of financial *unwellness* for a time. We can ignore it. Like a splinter that's just small enough to tolerate. But these issues have come crashing to the forefront (and into the workplace) during moments like the Great Recession or the COVID pandemic. These utterly unpredictable external shocks to market-driven events remind us that everything is interconnected—our physical, financial, and emotional wellness. Our lives and our livelihoods. They remind us that financial wellness is about far more than how much money we're able to divert to our 401(k)s each month, if any.

But in addition to the statistical realities and events that jar us and remind us of our financial fragility, a number of positive forces and game-changing megatrends are converging to accelerate interest and adoption of financial wellness solutions. We explore these in detail in Part III.

Leading voices on the bleeding edge of financial wellness

In addition to some employers who have been leading the way with financial wellness, several providers are doing an outstanding job of helping plan sponsors and participants think more broadly about financial wellness and make more informed decisions.

T. Rowe Price produces a tremendous amount of informative content about the individual financial journey and how employers can support it. Jellyvision has been at the forefront of educating participants with highly engaging, interactive decision support tools that help participants compare benefits and generally make the entire process of annual open enrollment more relatable, less clinical, and less uncertain. (You can read a bit more about Jellyvision on page 166). And Prudential, a household name, has made a very public commitment to the cause by completely rebranding around the concept of financial wellness.

Prudential's big pivot to financial wellness

Prudential has arguably the best financial wellness marketing campaign ever created. I love their outdoor billboards marketing all over the country. They remind us of some sobering truths:

"We spend more time thinking about retirement than planning for it."

"We spend more time rearranging our pictures on our iPhones than we do planning for retirement."

"We spend more time staring blankly into our refrigerators than we do planning for retirement."

The historically conservative 125-year-old Fortune 50 insurance company went all in on financial wellness in 2018. Not only did they create a spiffy ad campaign, they helped to define what financial wellness was and forever changed the arc of Prudential by telling the world (including its own employees and shareholders) in no uncertain terms that they were indeed a financial wellness company—one that just so happened to sell a whole lot of insurance and manage a whole lot of money.

Prudential completely rebranded around this idea and in 2018 launched "The Wellness Effect" by taking out a full-page ad in *The Wall Street Journal*. The video used to launch the program issued a call to employers: "Leaders from all sectors . . . must collaborate on finding ways to reconnect work and wealth."

What does this all signal? What should you even take from it and why should you read on? It tells us that financial wellness is no longer a nice-to-have, wish-list item for employers. The mandate for it is accelerating at warp speed. Our financial wellness as a society is declining, not improving. (And that's not just for the obvious segments of society. That's true even for highly educated executives who might look just like you, me, or our neighbors.) And we'll look in Part III at the fact that Millennials (and, again, maybe even you and me) are not at all convinced we'll be able to count on Social Security to even be there when we retire.

How do you know you need to do more to help employees with their financial wellness?

The need for financial wellness programs depends on the workforce, the industry, your brand promise, and other factors. But some of the more obvious symptoms that should get your attention include:

- Rising absenteeism
- Increase in sick time and health-care utilization/costs
- Falling billable productivity
- Computer usage patterns
- Dips in employee satisfaction
- Falling contributions to 401(k) and other savings vehicles
- Spikes in opt-out rates
- Increases in hardship withdrawals and 401(k) loan balances
- Distress-related calls to managers or HR service centers

What you stand to gain

Most employers know intuitively that it's the right thing to do. In a recent AON Hewitt study, a whopping 81 percent of respondents acknowledged this. And companies are starting to realize that not only is it the right thing to do, but it benefits productivity, morale, retention, and recruiting.

Fred Barstein, Founder and CEO of The Retirement Advisor University (TRAU) points out that, "We shifted so much of the burden to the employee, and I've never met one Millennial who thinks Social Security will be there for them. They grew up accustomed to having their hands held, and they need help."

It can advance your employer brand by:

- Making it easier to attract and retain talent.

- Helping you reduce other costs created by absenteeism, stress, distraction, and the costs of mental and physical health tolls that financial strain places on employees.

- Most importantly, it can demonstrate you're a true partner in the financial wellness of your employees. [3]

In Part II, we'll look a bit closer at some of the biggest hurdles to financial wellness, including the more massive burdens of student loan debt, credit card debt, health-care expenses, as well as the minor yet still hugely important factors such as housing expenses and the extensive weight of medical debt.

Questions to consider

- How are we defining financial wellness? Are we thinking as broadly as we could be about financial wellness?

- Do we have an actual strategy for financial wellness, or do we have a collection of employee benefits?

- For companies that may be competing for our talent, how are they approaching financial wellness? Why are we doing what we do?

- Relative to the financial wellness of our employees, what are the ideal outcomes for our business? For our employees?

- How do our financial wellness-related benefits support our diversity and inclusion strategy?

- Do we understand that 75 percent of our employee base is living with some sort of financial anxiety every day?

- Do we recognize that while the anxieties are the same, the solutions for different cohorts are different? One size does not fit all, which may be the case with many of our existing benefits.

- How are we showing our employees that we care about them as human beings, and how is that reflected in our financial and well-being strategy?

- Have we ever attempted to measure the impact that our employees' financial stress is having on our business? In terms of lost productivity, for example?

PART II—BIG ROCKS: OBSTACLES TO FINANCIAL WELLNESS

The truth is, there are countless obstacles standing between the American worker and true financial wellness. They can vary widely from person to person, family to family, region to region. But if we look at enough data, and talk to enough employers and workers, it becomes evident that some of these obstacles are much bigger and much more common than others. In this section, we examine the greatest obstacles impeding our path and look at ways we can roll up our sleeves and, together, move them out of the way and move on with our collective journey to financial wellness.

2

Student Loan Debt:
Our Failing Grade

*"May your college memories last as long as
your student loan payments."*

—Unknown

As a regular kid growing up in the 1980s, my sweet, well-intentioned parents with their lovely Welsh accents told me all I needed to do was work hard and get a good education and everything would work out. Millions of parents told their kids the same story, which they believed wholeheartedly. As I got older and reached university age, we all began taking out student loans like crazy, thinking we were doing the right thing.

By 2015, my friend, financial expert, former Governor of Indiana, and President of Purdue University Mitch Daniels warned that Americans had developed a dangerously "casual relationship" with student loan debt. He called it "a modern form of indentured servitude" and has been unrelentingly vocal about the broader negative impact of student loan debt on society as a whole.[1] A staunch critic of student loan debt and advocate for innovative programs such as income-share agreements between colleges, borrowers, and investors, Daniels was not the first expert to sound the alarm. But he has been a leading voice for reform, and I still find his summary among the most potent.

Our relationship with student loans has become dangerous and casual indeed.

As of 2020, there was roughly $1.7 trillion in student loan debt outstanding in the U.S., held by 45 million borrowers.[2] The average balance held by members of the class of 2018 alone is more than $29,000. Student loans also make up the largest chunk of non-housing debt in the U.S.[3]

And speaking of dangerous, this problem has been coming to a head for years, with more and more consumers taking out student loans only to find themselves trapped by them.

Student loan debt, especially when coupled with credit card debt, is one of the most draining, toxic forms of debt faced by American workers today. Especially younger workers.

BEHAVIOR NUDGES

Herding

People tend to do what others are doing. This can lead us to follow the crowd without first assessing whether things like student loans actually make sense for our own situation.

Approximately 75 percent of college graduates join the workforce saddled with student loan debt, making it the largest impediment facing younger Americans who are trying to begin their financial wellness journey, achieve financial independence, and launch "version 2.0" of their lives. And, yes, student loan debt is weighing down much of the workforce, including workers well into their thirties, forties, and those in their fifties. In some families, there may even be intergenerational student loan debt, where college-age kids are racking up debt while their parents are still struggling to pay off their own remaining student loans.

But it's those workers under age forty who carry the heaviest load. They're the ones employers need to be most concerned about. They need the most help, they're the largest modern demographic group, they're vocal, and they vote. Most importantly, study after study shows they heavily favor employers who are willing to step up and help them.

This reality creates both risk and opportunity for employers. Millennials now approaching their forties sign on each day stressed out and distracted by lingering student loans they thought they would have paid off already . . . not to mention the other obligations they may be juggling personally and professionally. And younger employees or job candidates are likely to show up on your doorstep dragging behind them thousands of dollars in student loan debt, proverbial anchors to what could or should have been an otherwise promising and unburdened career launch.

This can heavily color their career decisions. In the most obvious example, they may over-index on salary alone because they're so focused on weekly and monthly cash flow. They also gravitate to employers who offer some sort of student loan debt relief, with nine out of ten 2019 graduates reporting they were seeking an employer with student loan perks.

This will make it more costly for employers to woo and keep the best candidates when the labor market tightens (as it invariably will at some point). But it also makes the case for student loan debt relief as one of the top factors in hiring and retention.

In order for employers to be able to attract, hire, and retain the workforce of the future, and be employers of choice for any top candidates—but especially Millennials—employers will almost certainly have to offer student loan debt relief.

It's worth emphasizing that we aren't talking about tuition reimbursement here, or education or training expenses occurred on your behalf or for your benefit as the employer. I often see people confuse the two, so I always like to point that out.

We're talking about programs that help employees cope with preexisting or independently incurred student loan debt. These programs let employers make monthly contributions directly to an employee's retirement plan or loan servicer while employees continue to make regular payments. The monthly contribution, applied directly to principal, can shave several years off a loan and, if applied to the 401(k) plan, provides an incentive to pay off the loans even faster.

The current landscape

Student loan debt has been building to crisis levels for years. It boils down to this: students have borrowed huge amounts of money they couldn't possibly afford to pay back.

Under normal circumstances, consumers borrow money (for, say, a car or a home) based on credit history and proof of income (and maybe a cosigner). Makes perfect sense, right? But unlike other typical lending models, that's never really been the case with student loans. Instead, consumers have been allowed to borrow based on the cost of a particular college, irrespective of their actual ability to pay back a loan. It's been a recipe for disaster.

"You will be reincarnated six times. That's how long it will take to pay off your student loans."

Even prior to the economically devastating COVID-19 pandemic, employers, legislators, and fintech companies were starting to understand the gravity of the problem and offer solutions. The fact that it's now registering widely as a crisis is reflected in the fact that student loan repayment programs are gaining traction even more rapidly than 401(k) or HSA plans when they were first launched. The Society for Human Resource Management (SHRM) reported in 2019 that 8 percent of employers now offer student loan repayment programs. That number has doubled each year since 2016.[4]

Just as it has done for the entire topic of employee wellness, COVID has turned a hot spotlight on student loan debt specifically. It's brought the problem into sharp focus. In a matter of months, we accelerated our thinking and created a sense of urgency that would have otherwise taken years to coalesce.

Employers on the leading edge

Just five years or so ago, student loan repayment programs as an employee benefit were unheard of. Now they're central to the conversation. And employers who are offering them are seeing real business impact, not to mention the positive impact on employee experience and employer brand.

At OCC (Options Clearing Corporation), a Chicago-based equity derivatives clearinghouse, student loan assistance is the most-talked-about benefit at job fairs. Aetna offers a repayment benefit for employees who obtained undergraduate or graduate degrees within three years of applying. Staples offers its student loan program to sales associates and high performers. Peloton, a high flyer within the fitness and well-being space, offers its program to any employee with undergraduate or graduate-school loans, regardless of whether he or she obtained a degree.

Abbott Laboratories, one of the first movers in student loan debt relief, broke ground with their Freedom 2 Save program. In 2019, Abbott recognized a huge and growing problem among their workers, who were stressed out and struggling to manage student loan debt. Abbott successfully petitioned the IRS to make employer contributions to employee student loans tax deductible.

The result? One year after announcing the first-of-its-kind student loan employee benefit, more than one thousand Abbott employees signed up. The average amount of student loan debt held by each participant was $38,000.[5]

The IRS's decision to approve the plan on Abbott's behalf, now seen as a landmark ruling, is a loud and clear signal. It's a bellwether ruling in terms of what the future holds for student loan debt relief. My close friend Joseph Adams, partner at Winston & Strawn, represented his client, Abbott, and led the discussions with the Treasury Department and IRS. This program very smartly borrowed from the time-tested playbook of the 401(k) plan by automating the payroll deduction.

This groundbreaking program design approved by the IRS threw the doors wide open for other employers to follow suit. While the ruling narrowly applies to just one company at this time, it sets a precedent and is sure to have major implications in the future. It's also noteworthy because Abbott is a microcosm of American society as a whole: it has more than 107,000 employees, it's based in middle America, and it's in health care—one of the nation's largest, most influential industries. If their employees needed this kind of help, you could safely bet that millions of other employees across America would gratefully welcome a hand up from their employees in digging out from under their student loans.

In fact, the Abbott ruling has already influenced COVID-related relief enacted in early 2020—the CARES Act (see below)—and creates a solid and promising blueprint for how Congress will likely deal with student loan debt going forward.

Legislative remedies on the horizon

Federal legislation is also beginning to catch up by offering various short- and long-term remedies for student loan debt, often buried within bigger, more complex pieces of legislation. At the time of this writing, widespread talk of some form of student loan forgiveness is also surfacing and appears to be gaining steam. Exactly how it will play out remains to be seen, but the key point is the recognition student loans are getting as an obstacle to financial wellness.

The SECURE Act of 2019 allows families with 529 plans to use up to $10,000 tax-free per child to pay down student loans or to cover certain costs associated with registered apprenticeships (e.g., fees, textbooks, supplies and equipment, or tools required for the trades).[6] It is also the largest retirement reform to impact the economy since the Pension Protection Act of 2006,[7] which shored up protections for workers participating in pension plans and gave workers greater options for saving for their retirement. The mere fact that the Act addresses both student loans and retirement accounts shows how intertwined student loan debt relief and retirement planning are in our overall financial wellness.

The CARES Act, officially enacted in March 2020 to provide far-ranging relief from hardships resulting from the COVID-19 pandemic (colloquially referred to as the "PPP law" or "paycheck protection program"), recognized how student loans were amplifying the financial stress of American consumers as incomes fell and jobs rapidly disappeared. The Act carried a temporary provision that allowed employers to make tax-free payments of up to $5,250 toward their employees' student loans between March 27, 2020 and December 31, 2020. The employer payments could be excluded from employees' taxable income (as long as they went toward qualifying educational loans)—an important, even if temporary, win-win for both employer and employee.

It's also worth recognizing those few legislators who are incredibly instrumental in shaping wellness in the workplace solutions and have played an outsized role in helping Americans improve their financial and

"If Allen attends a $60,000 college for 48 months and borrows $240,000 in student loans at 7.9% interest, how long will it take him to steal someone's identity and move to a foreign country?"

subsequently life outcomes. Brian Graff, CEO of the American Retirement Association, says of Senator Rob Portman, Ohio (and, I might add, a fellow Dartmouth graduate), "Senator Portman has long been the most ardent advocate for the employee in terms of providing financial wellness solutions. He has a long history of framing the discussion on retirement plan design, leveraging the latest in behavioral finance thinking, and trying to lessen the financial anxiety burden on employees." Senator Portman has had a hand in the Pension Protection Act, Fiduciary Rule, Portman-Cardin Bill, the SECURE Act, and the CARES Act. His advocacy for consumers and workplace wellness shows up in two decades of legislation. Alas, however, Senator Portman will retire after his term is up in 2022. When that happens, this country and the American worker could use another fearless champion of financial wellness to step forward and fill his shoes.

Fintech solutions also on the rise

Companies that offer student loan repayment solutions have been cropping up left and right. While the space can seem overwhelming to employers, the good news is that there are many compelling options to choose from for those employers who do want to help employees address this problem.

The solutions can be remarkably easy to install and function like other payroll integration and deduction programs. Payroll processors already do that for thousands of benefits, well beyond payroll. Products have evolved quickly, as the fintech companies knew their student loan solutions had to be simple to implement for employers and employees to adopt them. The industry is expanding rapidly and currently includes players such as Gradifi Refi, Peanut Butter, Thrive, and Vault (formerly Student Loan Genius).

My friend Tony Aguilar founded the then-groundbreaking Student Loan Genius in June 2013. As a serial fintech entrepreneur and active voice in the Latino community, Tony was in the vanguard of the earliest employer-sponsored student loan repayment programs. One could argue that he was quite a bit ahead of his time, and that the marketplace wasn't quite ready to buy into the idea. (In fact, industry watchers like he and I, among others, have been advocating

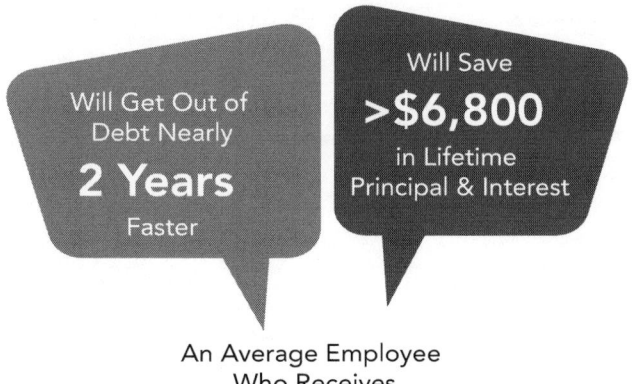

**An Average Employee
Who Receives**

$50/month

*Even a modest employer contribution toward student loan debt can make a huge
difference in the life—and loyalty—of an employee.*

Source: Peanut Butter

for student loan repayment programs for years.) But thinkers like Tony seeded the ground for these modern solutions. Much like my old clients Ask Jeeves, MySpace, Geocities, Beatnik, and other technologies that you've likely never heard of if you're under forty or so were arguably well ahead of their time. They were still visionary in offering real, often elegantly simple solutions that broke new ground and set the stage for subsequent innovation in the form of the current FAANG companies (Facebook, Amazon, Apple, Netflix, Google) and Spotify. Similarly, it's just taken a little while for these student loan debt repayment companies to begin to hit a critical mass in terms of recognizing the need, and now it seems they're well on their way to becoming a mainstream offering, as student loan debt is drawing more and more attention.

Now the company founded by Aguilar is known as Vault and owned by a number of financial and strategic partners, including Prudential and John Hancock. It's an integral part of the student loan landscape, as is Peanut Butter. I always thought "Peanut Butter" was an unusual name for a student loan software company, but it was chosen carefully. I asked my buddy, company Founder and CEO David Aronson, "So, Dave, what's with the name 'Peanut Butter'?" His response: "What was your go-to meal in college? For many of us, peanut butter was the only thing we could afford to eat. Our company's name is an homage to student debt holders everywhere."

It's true. There's no telling how many peanut butter sandwiches college students eat. Unfortunately, those who enter the workforce with any sizable student loan debt will probably continue eating them long after college if they've any hope of paying off their loans.

These tech-driven solutions draw directly on the power of the "nudge" phenomenon. Similar to a 401(k), they use automatic payroll deduction and employer contributions to push past human inertia—and incentivize people to do what's in their own best interests. It's a great example of human behavior, consumer demographics, technology, the expanding role of the employer, and public policy all intersecting to help employees make better decisions and move closer to financial wellness.

A look at the statistics

Countless statistics reveal just how big a problem student loan debt is in the U.S., and why it should matter to employers now:

1. The average amount of student loan debt has risen 86 percent in the past thirteen years.

2. Fifty-one percent of student loan holders say debt is ruining their quality of life.[8]

3. Fifty-four percent of Millennials don't have a retirement account.[9]

4. Eighty-seven percent of those in college or graduating this year with student debt say finding a company with a student loan benefit is important to them.

5. Eighty-six percent of employees (age twenty-one to thirty-six) state they would commit to an employer for five years in exchange for assistance paying off their student loans.[10]

6. Roughly one-third of employers expect to offer some form of student loan relief by 2021.[11]

Also telling regarding the weight of this burden is the poor repayment status of student loans. As student loan debt in the U.S. has grown, so too has the proportion of debt being postponed by borrowers. Only a little more than half of federally managed student loans are in repayment, according to data from the U.S. Department of Education (DOE). That leaves the remaining debt in various states of limbo, such as forbearance, deferment, grace period, or default. While these alternatives may give Millennials temporary relief, they each have future consequences—such as long-term damage to the borrower's credit score or interest that continues to pile up while making no progress against the principle—that will weigh on them and their families for years to come. Left unremedied, student loan debt truly has the power to ruin lives.

Historical context: how student loan debt blew up in our faces

How did student loan debt become such a problem for Millennials, in particular? In short, Millennials face the greatest student loan hardship than any previous generation because the cost of tuition has outpaced Gross Domestic Product (GDP) growth as they have come of age.

Simply put, the economy imploded in the early 2000s. The internet bubble burst, Enron and WorldCom failed, and 9/11 threw us into a tailspin very similar to what the COVID pandemic unleashed in 2020.

For decades prior to 2002, the cost of higher education and our GDP growth (the rate at which the U.S. economy grows each year) were in relative lockstep. For instance, if the economy was growing at 4 percent, then the cost of college grew at 4 percent. But after 2002, when our economy ground to a halt and we embarked on two wars abroad, higher education kept growing at a rate at which it pleased.

The bifurcation between those two key growth rates is the primary reason the cost has significantly outpaced our country's growth rate, wage inflation, and the ability of average Americans to afford a four-year college degree. This also coincided with the first year in which Millennials entered the workforce. So virtually all outsized student loan debt has been shouldered by this generation. While many complicating factors led to the explosion of student loan debt, these were two of the most powerful.

Not only was their cost of higher education greater than preceding generations, Millennials took on 300 percent more student loan debt than their parents did. Millennials were also sorely lacking in financial literacy, in an increasingly complicated financial world that now included multiple debt obligations, the need for emergency fund planning, and retirement planning decisions and pressures. This added up to the perfect storm:

- College expenses were rising rapidly and at a much higher rate than other household expenses.

- We were in the throes of a recession, and tuition rates were rising faster than the GDP.

- The federal government was subsidizing and lending most of the fairly easy money at temptingly low rates.

- Bank deregulation made it easy for banks to offer Millennials truckloads of money by writing loans they didn't need with rates and amounts they couldn't really afford.

- Millennials took the easy money and sometimes used it for expenses other than tuition.

One key culprit: the dysfunctional business of higher education

The truth is that, prior to the 2020 COVID-19 pandemic, which shined a glaring light on the delivery of higher education, higher education was one of the only industries that had not been forced to innovate, rationalize costs, or reallocate resources in recent years. It's basically been a multi-decade, expanding heyday of increased costs for tuition, building, housing, and curriculum for higher education. Just consider the endowments of Stanford, Harvard, Yale, and Princeton. Ironically, they tend to invest

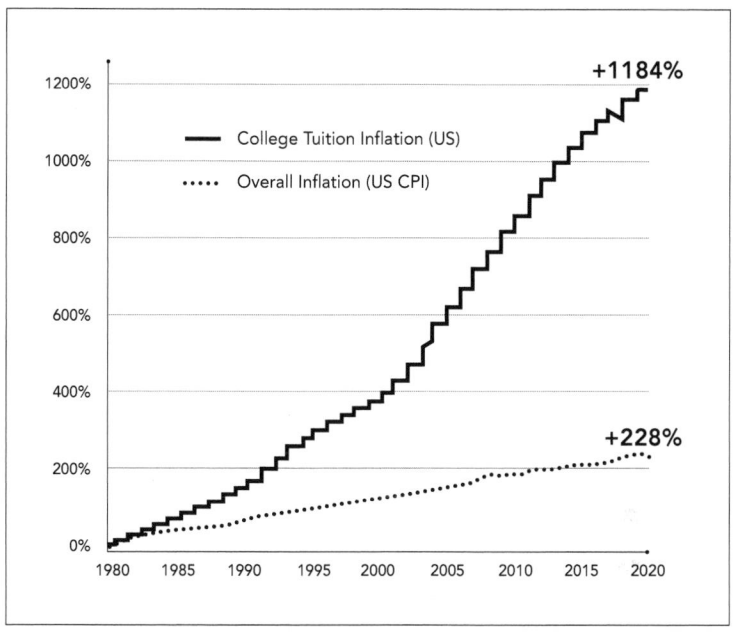

Source: US Bureau of Labor Statistics

For years now, college tuition costs have risen relatively unheckaed and at a much higher rate than the regular inflation rate.

heavily in venture capital (VC) funds that fuel those very same fintech advancements, such as student loan repayment platforms, that address the very problem created by the loans taken out so students could afford to attend these institutions.

I don't want to pick on higher education too much here, as it plays such a vital role in society. But if we're being intellectually honest and we're sincere about trying to help people, does it make sense for colleges and universities to continue defining success based on fundraising results or how many new buildings they can erect? Could we not use more of those resources to at least rationalize expenses in a more disciplined way and lower the cost even a little bit? Does it make sense to raise all this money for financial aid, then reward it on a blind basis (rather than based on actual need)?

If we think back to 2016, when even Malcolm Gladwell started asking— in his "Revisionist History" podcast—some incredibly tough questions about how higher education was spending money and the absurdity of the size of many college endowments (which will likely never be touched, at least not directly, to improve student outcomes or lower tuition costs), we have to agree that these are extremely valid, even if uncomfortable, questions.

Public universities have also continued to raise tuition. From 2008 to 2018, the average tuition at four-year public colleges increased by 37 percent, while their net costs increased by only 24 percent. During that same time, forty-one states spent 13 percent less per student.[12]

So, while it's tempting to just blame consumers for their predicament, we also have to look at the role of the institutions themselves if we're to make a remotely honest assessment of the student loan debt crisis in America. Like so many things in the world of banking and investments, it's enough to make even so-called experts scratch their heads.

Behavioral science experts like bestselling author Dan Ariely, and James B. Duke, Professor of Psychology and Behavioral Economics at Duke University, and Kristen Berman, Cofounders of Irrational Labs, have called on higher education to offer solutions to the problem. In Berman's words, "Sure, getting a college degree seems the logical thing to do for your future income. But we have a systematic problem. We need to figure out how to offer education at a lower cost." It's an enormous oxymoron, given higher education's role as a cradle of innovation. A cradle of academic innovation, perhaps, but not a cradle for operational innovation that delivers greater value for their parent and student buyers.

Berman adds, "Much like excessive lending and the housing bubble, we have had a system that encourages people to buy things that they don't need. Even if they qualify for scads of loans, we need to figure out a way to offer people as little as possible. So college isn't a user problem, but a system problem. Taking as much as you're offered isn't necessarily good."

To date, there have been half-step measures in which higher education is merely raising more money and reallocating it to student financial aid. But this isn't facing or fixing the underlying issues. The only way this problem has any hope of being solved is if the institutions themselves come to the table and are willing to embrace true change.

To some degree, the innovations forced by COVID in online learning and alternative delivery have begun to affect how higher education operates, but it remains to be seen if there will be any fundamental systemic changes. They'll have no choice; they can't charge the same for remote classes as they were for the full, on-campus experience. Plus, even before COVID, elite private universities across the country were already facing budget deficits that have only continued to grow. That's not sustainable. A seismic change in higher education is happening, and some now believe it's been accelerated.

But it's far from fair to lay all the blame at the feet of higher ed and lenders. Charles Wheelan, Senior Lecturer, Author, and Policy Fellow at Dartmouth College, wryly points out, "We love borrowing for what it allows us to do—until we can't pay it back. And we love bankers who make it possible—until we want to pelt them with stones."

The burden for employees

Employees or candidates with any notable amount of student loan debt can be utterly trapped.

Because of the timing and circumstances outlined above, Millennials carry the heaviest load of all. If they fail to service the debt, they can impair their credit and ruin the opportunity to borrow strategically for other life needs. If, on the other hand, they prioritize repayment of student loans, it can drain cash flow and render them unable to save money for a house, car, childcare, children's tuition or, most importantly, retirement. It's a fact that you can't wait until the eleventh hour to save for retirement. It also leaves them with little to no free cash to contribute to tax-advantaged financial instruments such as health savings accounts (HSAs). It's a conundrum that, unfortunately, Millennials in particular are ill-equipped to handle on their own.

So, many employees who are busy servicing student loans have little or nothing left to contribute to retirement savings. Many are forced to delay major life choices and capstone events—home ownership, car purchases or other purchases, even marriage or starting or growing a family—because so much of their pay is sucked up by student loan obligations. All of the data bears this out as truth.

For Millennials especially, student loan debt is sucking the oxygen out of the room and draining most of their available cash flow. As much as any other form of debt, student loan debt robs them of the freedom to make intentional, strategic decisions about their personal finances, life priorities, and their careers. It's a huge obstacle standing between employees, financial wellness, and their own idea of the American Dream.

Opportunities for employers

Student loan debt as a topic of conversation was already moving to the forefront before the COVID pandemic. Now it's been pushed front and center, as we've been reminded of just how big a strain it's placing on American workers. Employers have also taken a step back, become more empathetic, and realized workers really do need their help. And workers want this benefit.

I believe employers who don't do something to help employees with their student loan debt do so at their own peril. It's not uncommon for our team to present to some executives who roll their eyes when I suggest they offer some sort of student loan debt relief. They ask, "Why should we invest in that?" or insist, "It's not our problem that some Millennial doesn't know how to handle money." Study after study tells us this is an outdated view. If you don't offer this benefit to your employees, especially your Millennial employees, another employer will.

Student loan repayment assistance programs do far more than just give employees measurable relief from one of their greatest financial stressors. Employers benefit significantly, as well:

- Speed of hiring increases by 13 percent

- Average employee tenure increases by 36 percent

- Employers gain wider access to talent, given that 85 percent of candidates would accept a job offer with an employer that offers student loan repayment

Other strategic benefits to consider:

Student loan debt remediation helps minority employees and can foster diversity and inclusion efforts in a meaningful way. According to Peanut Butter, student loan debt places a disproportionate strain on minorities. Roughly two-thirds of student debt is held by women, and Blacks and Hispanics are twice as likely to hold student debt as their White peers. All three of those groups take longer to repay student loans and are more likely to default. African American borrowers pay their education debt down at just 4 percent each year, a full 6 percent lower than their White peers. With these numbers, researchers in the study mentioned previously concluded that roughly a quarter of the Black–White wealth gap was due to student debt.

Further supporting this idea, a 2019 Abbott Laboratories survey revealed that 70 percent of Black and 76 percent of Hispanic Americans with student loan debt say finding an employer with a student loan debt employee benefit is important, and almost half of each group (49 percent and 47 percent, respectively) say it's "very important."

Student loan repayment programs can set your employer brand apart

By acting now, employers can take advantage of a rare window of differentiation, broaden their recruiting options, and get in front of legislative pressure that's almost certain to come in the near future.

You have ample vendor partner options. There is a rapidly growing number of reputable fintech partners who can help your company define and implement a program. They can help you look across your employee segments and offer a program that works best for your workforce. And don't let yourself get overwhelmed with options. The industry is young and dynamic; it will continue to consolidate. That's OK. It's more important to act than to agonize and lose time trying to arrive at the most perfect answer.

Setting up a loan repayment program can be easier and more cost effective than you might assume. Consider hiring a consultant or advisor to help you make an objective assessment and navigate the request for proposal (RFP) process and implementation. They can also help you optimize an existing program. You could consider running a pilot program with part of your employee base; it doesn't have to be an all-or-nothing proposition. The best news for employers, as mentioned in the Introduction, is that bidirectional integration and payroll automation have evolved to a point where offering some form of loan repayment solution can truly be a no-brainer of an offering for most employers.

The business case for student loan repayment

- ✓ State and federal income taxes no longer need to be withheld for contributions. **A tax savings of about $0.30/dollar goes directly to the employee's bank account.**

- ✓ **Save on payroll taxes.** Your company no longer needs to withhold FICA, FUTA, or SUTA for contributions. **A tax savings of about $0.10/dollar stays on the company's balance sheet and improves earnings.**

Source: https://www.getpeanutbutter.com/tax-free-2021/

The most important takeaway is this: *Student loan debt assistance is no longer just a "nice-to-have" benefit.*

Employers are offering this benefit at a rapidly increasing rate, and the time to act is now. It's a cornerstone financial wellness benefit that will determine winners and losers in the zero-sum game of talent attraction and retention. We speak with thousands of HR and finance executives each year, and the number offering these initiatives only continues to grow.

Dave Aronson, Founder of Peanut Butter, Inc., views it this way: "Student loan delays what many of us envision as the American Dream. If an employer helps out, there's a win-win for the employer and employee together. For employers, it's about creating and capturing value. That's the opportunity HR departments have with student loans. There's value to be created by engaging, attracting, and retaining people with debt."

A glimpse of the future

One of the most drastic transformations we may see could be in the business of higher education itself. The entire industry may look completely different in the near future.[13] A 2020 article in *Financial Advisor* said simply that, in the post-COVID era, "College education won't look like what it did before. People will now be asking what the return on their investment is—what are the value proposition and cost benefits, exactly? Would you want to spend $150,000 on an education and go into debt and then become an elementary educator or do social work? Might a cheaper associate degree or state college education give you a better value?" The industry was already under pressure to innovate, and COVID has only amped up that pressure.

Additionally, employers will continue to embrace their pivotal role in financial wellness and will use ever-advancing technology—including AI—to offer highly tailored, creative, cost-effective solutions to their employees' student loan debt challenges. Many larger companies, especially those with strong tax and legal teams, will also follow Abbott Laboratories. They'll move ahead and offer student loan debt repayment, knowing that the precedent set by Abbott means that the IRS would also allow them to treat the contributions to employees as tax deductible.

More importantly, widespread legislation designed to directly address student loan debt is sure to continue gaining steam. Groundbreakers like Mitch Daniels of Purdue University, Professor Lesley Turner of Vanderbilt University, and Rob Portman (one of the early Congressional voices in the wilderness calling for employer-sponsored solutions) and others who truly understand the problem are likely to continue pushing for relief that creates a win-win for both borrowers and employers.

All these factors combined will very likely result in a workplace-driven solution for student loan debt that becomes as widely available and adopted as the 401(k) plan. It will be tax deductible for employers and employees, automated, and will take advantage of the behavior "nudges" (with automatic enrollment and payroll deduction) that made 401(k) plans such a huge success.

Above all, forward-thinking, outcome-based solutions driven by business and political leaders who really understand the problem will be key to ultimately tackling this mountain of debt. Like any problem, the ingenuity of American society will drive meaningful innovation in the delivery and pricing of higher education. More importantly, it will devise a wide array of solutions to help employees break the chains of student loan debt and move closer to true financial wellness.

But in the meantime, the problem of student loan debt is very big and very real. While higher education slowly evolves and legislation inches forward, it is employers who are and will remain perfectly positioned to offer real solutions to the greatest numbers of consumers right now and in the future.

Questions to consider

- What percentage of our employees are Millennials?

- Given that the number of employers offering some sort of student loan debt relief has doubled each year for the past five years, have we discussed this possibility in a meaningful way?

- What percentage of our employees have student loan debt?

- Have we evaluated specific student loan debt solutions for our employees?

- Do we realize just how easy payroll deduction programs are to implement?

- Do we know what our competitors are doing to help employees manage student loan debt?

- Have our employees expressed interest or need in getting some form of help managing their student loan debt?

- Do we understand just how much more our employees could be saving for retirement if they could knock out any student loan debt?

- Are we aware of the Abbot case study and have we discussed how it might apply to our business?

- Is our management team fully aware that Millennials consider student loan debt relief to be the most important workplace benefit?

- Do we know the approximate total amount of student loan debt our employees are carrying?

- Are members of our management team resistant to offering student loan debt solutions to employees? If so, why?

3

CREDIT CARD OVERHANG: THE SLIPPERY SLOPE

"What can be added to the happiness of a man who is in good health, out of debt, and has a clear conscience?"

—Adam Smith, Scottish economist

In the world of rock climbing, "overhang" refers to a rock face that sits at an angle of greater than 90 degrees from the ground. Overhangs are enticing to many climbers because of the challenge they present in defying gravity. But they can be tricky, even downright dangerous, for even the most seasoned veterans of the sport to navigate in their climb to the summit. It can be hard to find a handhold or a foothold on overhangs. They're tiring. Pieces of rock can break free. Their sharp edges can cut safety ropes, sending a climber into freefall.

Like these perilous features found in nature, credit card overhang is one of the biggest, most jagged, and most dangerous impediments sitting between American workers and financial wellness.

Our chronic addiction to credit cards

One of the most toxic modern financial realities is our infatuation with and reliance on credit cards. Cards that come in all shapes, sizes, weights, colors, denominations, spending limits, interest rates, and tempting loyalty program packages.

Most of us know intuitively that American society has a near-schizophrenic relationship with credit cards. We know they can be a trap, yet we love the convenience and perks they offer—even when they have hefty annual fees and high interest rates. As one of countless internet memes says, we toggle between "I need to save money and YOLO."

What makes it even more challenging is that, even when we freeze our credit reports in hopes of avoiding fraud and unsolicited offers, we're still being marketed to constantly one way or another.

We're encouraged by credit card issuers to form bad habits that can be incredibly difficult to break. It's an interesting and schizophrenic relationship we have with cards—and that banks and other card issuers have even with themselves.

On the one hand, it seems they genuinely want us to have financial wellness and peace of mind. Sure, they offer advice-based content on how to manage credit card debt and offer the occasional improvements to statements or online views to help us see interest expense more clearly. Yet it sometimes seems they only want consumers to remain solvent enough to keep spending and carrying balances to the brink without defaulting.

All too frequently, people incur debt just to accumulate award miles, reward points, upgrades, free flights to Boston, or roundtrip flights at the end of the year, just to maintain their status. Maybe you've done it yourself. Or we convince ourselves to pay for things like utilities and groceries on our cards to drive as much spending as possible through the rewards "machine."

Credit cards as a safety net for essential purchases

On the other end of the spectrum from those who use credit cards only for discretionary purchases are the 40 percent of everyday Americans who feel forced to use a credit card because they're barely making ends meet and need a way to purchase basic necessities. So, we know for that segment of the population, living paycheck to paycheck, credit cards serve a valuable short-term solution to pay for essentials such as groceries, utilities, childcare, or car repairs. However, there are huge consequences to routinely charging anything to your credit card, regardless of the reason.

What happens if you hit an unexpected bump? You meant to pay the balance in full. But, oops, you have to roll that balance over. Say you hit another bump, run late with a payment, and get slapped with a rate increase. It doesn't take much to get swept up in the credit card spiral. Or to stick with our opening metaphor, that overhang can get steeper and more severe before we ever realize it.

A few years ago, I had my wallet stolen and had to replace my credit cards. I had several big-name cards, and cards from Home Depot, Lowe's, Dick's Sporting Goods, Sports Authority (incidentally, now bankrupt)—as well as for retailers I hadn't purchased from in years. Every now and then I'd take pity on a long-unused, lonely card and buy something to keep the account open "just in case." To think I was feeling sorry for *them*!

I generally despise shopping, so I took the opportunity to pare back to a manageable number . . . which, in hindsight, was still an absurd number. Just ask my kids: I have an extremely limited set of DIY skills, so the fact that I had *any* cards of a hardware superstore variety is, well, how do you say it—yes, absurd.

And if I'm a financial expert and behavioral finance disciple and this is *my* confession, imagine how everyday consumers wrestle with their love-hate relationship with cards.

Historical perspective: an industry formed over centuries

The history of credit and credit cards is fascinating. Humans have used credit instruments for centuries. Issuance of credit can be dated back to at least 3500 BC Sumeria. Historians have found evidence of credit arrangements on papyrus, in Sanskrit, and in the Code of Hammurabi, which set limits on interest rates and required credit agreements to be witnessed and added to the public record.[1] Card-like credit accounts and instruments, such as imprintable personal plates, were in use and have been evolving nonstop since before the birth of our nation. The Bible even speaks to rules and follies surrounding borrowing and the charging of interest, in books ranging from Deuteronomy to Proverbs.

And many readers may not know or remember this, but there was a time when it was extremely hard to get a credit card such as American Express. In its early days, underwriting requirements were strict, and the balance had to be paid each month. And before credit cards, there used to be things called traveler's checks—does that ring a distant bell?

There are many more fun details we could cover on the history of cards, but the key point is that in the most recent past there has been rapid, explosive proliferation of store-specific cards, bank-issued cards, and technology advances that have all made it easier to get and use cards. Statistics and hard evidence aside, we know from just living and functioning in society that credit cards have become loose, free, and easy to obtain in the past twenty years or so.

Anecdote alone is enough: who doesn't know first- or second-hand the sad, stress-inducing story of someone $30k in debt on a $40k salary? Banks play a major role in this, as they have gone from being safe havens and beacons of stewardship to fee-generating machines that count on consumers to overlook the fine print and make decisions that are *not* in their own best interests.

Legislation has failed to keep pace, much less prevent the current epidemic

If we look at a few milestones, we see there has been no real movement to rein in the industry. And some legislation has made the problem worse. In fact, credit card debt rose due to the Bankruptcy Protection Act of 2005. The Act made it harder for people to file for bankruptcy. As a result, they turned to credit cards as a stopgap. Credit card debt reached $1.028 trillion in July 2008. That was an average of $8,640 per household; unfortunately, much of it comprised of medical expenses (see Chapter 4).[2]

The Great Recession of 2008 curtailed credit card debt, which fell more than 10 percent in each of the first three months of 2009.[3] During that recession, banks cut back on consumer lending. Then the Dodd-Frank Wall Street Reform Act tightened regulations over credit cards. It also created the Consumer Financial Protection Agency to enforce those regulations. In addition, banks tightened credit standards. By April 2011, credit card debt had fallen to a low of $839.6 billion. Despite these decreases, the average American household still owed $7,055 each.

In 2009, the Credit Card Accountability Responsibility and Disclosure Act of 2009 (or Credit CARD Act) was the most significant legislation governing the credit card industry in decades. It was put in place to protect consumers against unfair practices. Today the CARD Act, as it's commonly known, protects consumers in numerous ways:

- Issuers could no longer raise rates without notifying consumers.

- Over-limit fees were capped.

- Card issuers were stopped from granting new accounts to anyone under twenty-one without an adult cosigner or proof of ability to pay.

- Required credit card issuers to remain at least one-thousand feet away from college campuses if they were offering any type of gift to students in exchange for a completed card application.

Through the lens of time, these actions seem paltry given the amount of credit card debt today, and many of them have done little to curtail questionable practices or dampen spending. It's also interesting that it assumes those over twenty-one have a clearer understanding of financial literacy, budgeting, and planning than those under age twenty-one. We know that's simply not the case.

The current landscape

Today, credit cards are extremely easy to get, regardless of your age, credit history, or income. And sadly, other than a few actions such as the Fair Credit Reporting Act, legislation has failed to keep pace with the fact that humans need protection from both themselves and card issuers. Worse, we have a credit reporting and scoring system that often punishes consumers for closing credit accounts, even ones in good standing.

While there has been a crackdown on certain industries like predatory payday lenders or punishing fines slapped on credit companies that have had data breaches, in contrast little has been done to regulate the free and easy issuance of credit cards, and the lack of understanding of the issues of accumulating balances and compounding interest expense. This has left consumers essentially naked, afraid, and stuck in a spin cycle of credit card usage.

The statistics

Statistics, factoids, and studies abound regarding credit card debt. At the time of this writing alone, a Google search for credit card debt yields 308,000,000 results. But it only takes a handful to give us some quick sizing on the problem:

- Groceries are the number-one reason consumers carry a credit card balance.[4]

- Forty-eight percent of card users make only minimum payments each month.[5]

- The typical American holds four credit cards, and credit card issuers are giving Americans more room to run up debt, boosting the typical credit limit by 20 percent over the last decade, to $31,000.[6]

- Upwards of 75.5 percent of consumers have at least one credit card.[7]

- Between 1991–2020, credit card interest rates averaged between 11.82 percent and 18.28 percent.[8]

- The average cash transaction is $22, while the average noncash transaction is $112.[9]

- The average credit card balance per person in the United States was $6,194 in 2019—an increase of 3 percent compared to 2018.[10]

- Seventy-five percent of consumers who have one or more credit cards carry an average credit card balance over $6,200. Average total balances above $6,200 have grown 3 percent over the past five years.[11]

- The country's outstanding credit card and other types of revolving debt have jumped 20 percent from a decade ago, reaching an all-time high of about $1.1 trillion.[12]

Spotlight on Gen Xers

Gen X, the generation between the Boomers and Millennials, has struggled along with Millennials and others. This segment carries more credit card debt than any other generation, with fifty-one-year-old consumers having the highest average credit card balance: $8,658.[13] Notwithstanding the following chart, however, Gen Xers are older, have a higher household income, and have typically already begun to focus in earnest on their retirement plans. Likewise, Gen Xers also don't have the crippling amount of student loan debt Millennials have. This alone makes the credit card debt—while not ideal—much more manageable, as they are basically naturally maturing (or, you could argue, being forced) into better financial decision-making and healthier relationships with credit cards.

Spotlight on Millennials

The Millennial generation has been hit the hardest by unemployment, lack of savings, and two recessions during their relatively short careers.[14] While we might assume student loan debt to be the primary concern for this cohort, it certainly isn't the only problem. More than half (51.5 percent) of Millennial respondents to most surveys have credit-card debt.[15] Outside student loan debt, credit cards

BEHAVIOR NUDGES

Overconfidence

People tend to believe they are right and that they are above average. This can affect every area of our lives. For example, we may take out credit cards or buy-now-pay-later financing, thinking we can easily pay it back later.

are the biggest chunk of debt for this group, yet 22 percent don't even know the interest rates on their cards. And while nearly 68 percent have some or a lot of stress about it, around 30 percent have little to no stress at all. This is the worst of all scenarios: they're in trouble, yet highly confident their financial house is in order. We see a similar phenomenon as people enter retirement. Many are absolutely confident they are fine, when in fact they have false hopes and dreams not backed with any sort of plan. Hope and prayer, while good for many things, is not a financial plan.

As Millennials have matured, some of their spending seems to have been tempered a bit, but it certainly hasn't stopped. Instead, during periods like

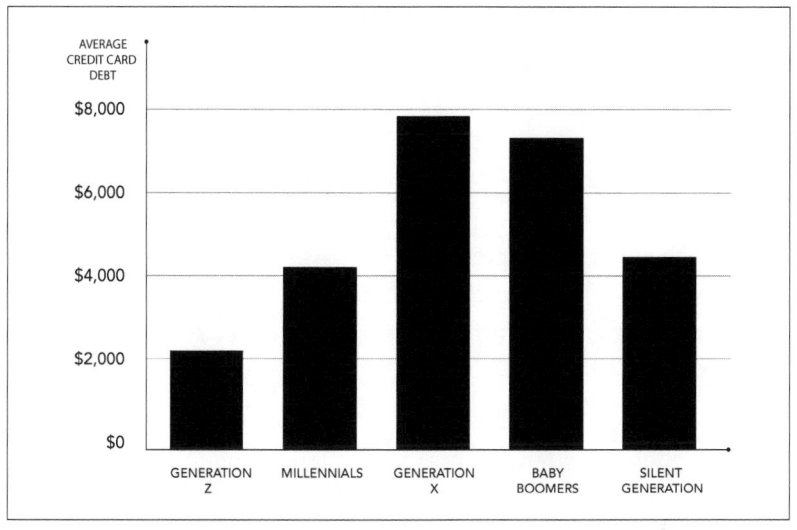

No generation is immune from credit card debt. Even Gen Z is already making use of credit cards.

COVID, they seem to have substituted experiential spending for things like home renovations or upgrades or RVs.

There literally is no end to the studies and stats, but the bottom line is that credit cards will continue to be used, although the ability to use them wisely will make a key difference in a person's ability to achieve any semblance of financial wellness. More importantly, there are sound alternatives to credit cards. Consumers just need help identifying what those are and why they make sense.

The challenge for employees

Employees are a microcosm of society.

As an employer, you can bank on the fact that a large portion of your employee base is losing sleep at night over credit card debt. They may be rolling over ever-expanding balances, making only minimum payments, and biting at every new card offer they get . . . or worse yet, they may become so numb or tired that they see credit card balances as the norm. They don't know just how stressed they should be by that interest expense they're racking up every month.

Behavioral finance: sometimes used against us

For all the highly respected, independent behavioral finance experts out there trying to warn and educate consumers, there are just as many of them out there working on behalf of credit card companies. Their job is to help credit card companies entice you into spending and carrying balances each month. That can leave consumers utterly confused or almost hypnotized into using credit cards constantly. (In Chapter 8, we explore this industry further.)

Even down to the very design and materials used for cards, card issuers do everything they can to make cards look good, imply status, sit nicely in your wallet, and feel good in your hands. Who hasn't gotten a little sizzle of delight from receiving that gorgeous new replacement card with a beautiful design or titanium feel? Trust me, I know. Designers within the walls of card issuers spend hours, weeks, and months creating design options before a new card design ever sees the light of day.

We're being duped. It's not hopeless, but it is bleak because so much of the burden is on consumers. If you miss a mortgage payment or rent, there are audible alarms and painful consequences. But with cards, the system has silenced the alarms, essentially making it easier and easier to spend more and more.

All this lulls us into thinking only in the moment, emotionally and transactionally, rather than strategically.

In many cases, this is coupled with the student loan debt we examined in Chapter 2, making it nearly impossible for employees to summon the discipline and cash flow needed to find their way to any sort of financial wellness.

It's also important to bear in mind that while this chapter focuses mainly on traditional credit card debt, employees may also be caught in the loop of using contractor-offered credit solutions for things like home repairs.

Before they know it, even the smartest, most level-headed employee can end up saddled with massive debt, much of which may come from credit cards and credit accounts. That calm-seeming colleague or member of your team may have credit outstanding all over the place.

Employees may be precariously overleveraged, to put it in business terms.

BEHAVIOR NUDGES

Planning Fallacy

People consistently underestimate how long things will take and how many resources they will require. This can lead us to have tunnel vision as we make a range of decisions, from credit card usage, homebuying decisions, and more.

And it's a truly vicious cycle.

Every dollar they're spending on credit cards is money they're not deploying to pay down a student loan, plowing into an emergency fund, or contributing to retirement. And while they might be master jugglers, what happens when the music stops? A $1,000 spending spree on that card can turn into $1,875 in just twenty-four months, even if the minimum monthly payment is made. No bueno. And if you look at a moment in time like the COVID pandemic, the innate resiliency of the consumer and willingness to just keep buying on credit is great for the economy, but terrible for individuals.

Even minor missteps with one credit card can harm a credit score, while anything more serious can choke off access to reasonably priced capital when it's really needed most. And cash flow that's constantly diverted to credit card debt interferes with the ability to save enough to allow us the freedom to "choose your day" (something we often say at Sheridan Road

Financial to denote true financial freedom), the ability to deploy cash flow more productively, or even retire on our own terms.

Opportunities for employers

Unless your employees have almost super-human self-control, (which they don't), they likely have some sort of credit card debt. Even the most rational cardholder might give in to splurge spending now and then. Maybe they just wrapped up a huge project and need a mental health week on a tropical island. Or maybe they want to travel cross-country to propose marriage. "Why would we drive six hundred miles one way? Blow through cash we ain't made? Why does a man do anything in the whole damn world? Cause there's a girl." As country crooner Trent Harmon says, emotions like love or stress can cause even the best of us to justify spending sprees. But the truth is, this sort of spending (on experiences or material items) does nothing to improve anyone's financial wellness.

Employers offer one of the last bastions of hope and protection against an industry that masterfully encourages consumers to spend money they don't have and carry balances each month. Now, more than ever, employers can help employees understand credit card debt and find ways to minimize it.

Left to their own devices, employees may not have the means nor the will to reduce their use of credit cards. "Employers have woken up to the fact that a majority of workers are having a lot of trouble simply getting by, never mind getting ahead," says Liz Davidson, Founder and CEO of Financial Finesse, one of the pioneers in the world of workplace financial education and wellness.

By offering educational programming and concrete solutions as part of your benefits lineup, you can make a difference in the lives of employees and shore up your ability to attract and retain the best talent. And even more importantly, by taking steps to offer options that help employees think more critically and allow them to fund life expenses through alternate solutions such as Kashable, short-term emergency payroll loans or advances, you can go a long way to helping them reduce stress, cut ties with credit cards, lower the interest rates from which they are borrowing, free up cash flow for savings and retirement, and move closer to financial nirvana.

A growing number of companies are helping workers gain access to payroll advances and loans, reflecting growing awareness and concern over the impact money problems are having on productivity levels and worker retention. Employers including Walmart, Facebook, Boeing, and JP Morgan have recently added these services. The aim is to help cash-strapped employees, many with damaged credit, cover unexpected expenses without resorting to high-cost debt.

Workers typically access the services online. The payroll-advance programs generally give employees the option to accelerate a portion of their next paycheck for a fee that often amounts to a few dollars. The loans are typically a couple thousand dollars and are repaid through automatic payroll deductions over a few months to a year or longer. Approval and interest rates, generally 6 to 24 percent, often depend on salary, tenure, and the amount of the loan or advance.

A number of fintech companies are emerging to fill this gap in employer-sponsored financial wellness solutions. However, large leading-edge record keepers such as Fidelity and Prudential currently have yet to select and offer a payroll loan program. The jury is still out on these programs as to their efficacy, and whether they're in fact nudging behavior in the right direction or simply enabling a different kind of poor decision-making. Typically, much like an employee assistance program (EAP) that is packaged, embedded, and offered as part of a company benefits program, these tools are, in fact, offered by separate third-party companies, with names like Kashable, Salary Finance, OnWard, True Connect, Vault, and HoneyBee. They typically are at no risk or cost to the employer and give employees access to a regulated bank loan without requiring a credit check.

These companies have followed a similar trajectory as other financial wellness and student loan repayment technologies since their founding: startup, venture capital funding, a period of education, and maturation, before finally realizing that employers are often the best distribution channels for these technologies. In fact, both Kashable and Vault were founded in 2013 and only really since 2018 have they begun to find their way on to broad-based distribution platforms.

But each employer will have to weigh out the best way to help employees. Ken Verzella, Vice President at Empower and former Chief Strategist of FInancial Wellness at Mass Mutual, poses a provocative and interesting question about employer-sponsored solutions that involve lending money and providing a way out of the credit card addiction. He asks, "Are we sending the wrong message by offering these services? Are employers just enabling borrowing behavior?" He adds, "Companies should be helping employees build good habits of saving, spending, and borrowing when and where appropriate. By offering these solutions, employers risk doing nothing more than making it even easier and frictionless to have money advanced to them."

To him, it's not really a loan as much as a payroll advance with interest. It also begs the question that employees may develop the same instincts to routinely borrow as much as they can from employer sources, as we see routinely in those who borrow from their 401(k) as an example. But regardless of the solutions that may be available in the marketplace, each employer must consider their employer brand promises; their internal corporate and social responsibility; their mission, vision, and values; and the needs of their workforce, then determine if these alternative solutions will legitimately and ultimately advance the financial well-being of individual employees.

Questions to consider

- Without doing any research, do I know offhand the exact interest rates on each of my credit cards? Can our employees answer this question about their own credit cards?

- Beyond the provision to borrow from their retirement savings, have we evaluated or are we offering other lending solutions that might help employees minimize or at least better manage their credit card usage when they have tight cash flow (e.g., emergency/cash savings tools, payroll advances at fair rates, etc.)?

- Do we offer any options through a credit union, such as cash savings, payroll advances, or something other than credit cards?

- Are we offering any education on the perils of accumulating credit card debt?

- What can we do to change our employees' behavior and the relationship they have with their credit cards?

MEDICAL DEBT:
AN EXTRAORDINARY PROBLEM
FOR ORDINARY PEOPLE

*"Financial ruin from medical bills is almost exclusively
an American disease."*

—Roul Turley, Author

You don't have to be an expert to know we could devote an entire book—or hundreds of books—to this topic alone.

The entire issue of health insurance is immense, complicated, and often controversial. It's one of the thorniest issues employers face in trying to run a profitable business.

While the topic of student loan debt can often dominate headlines as the biggest impediment to financial wellness, we can't ignore the dark role that extraordinary and unforeseen medical-related debt plays in holding us back from financial wellness. Medical debt caused by gaps in health-care coverage afflicts legions of people each year, turns their financial and emotional houses upside down, leads to personal bankruptcies, and can destroy a person's ability to retire as planned.

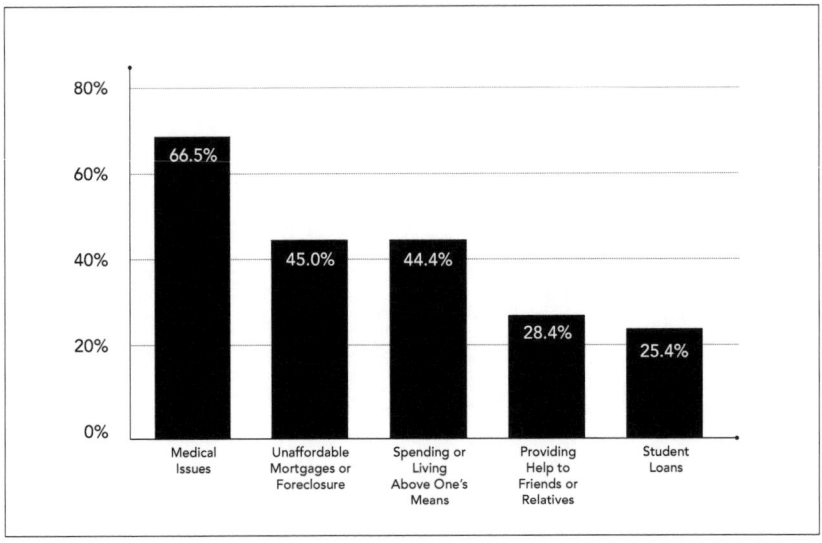

https://www.businessinsider.com/causes-personal-bankruptcy-medical-bills-mortgages-student-loan-debt-2019-6

Medical issues are by far the leading cause of personal bankruptcy in the U.S. This might stem from bills not covered by insurance, lost work income, or other issues related to illness or a medical emergency.

Often, as HR and financial professionals, we talk about "extraordinary" medical expenses when it comes to a costly medical event. But the truth is, a rather ordinary accident or event can quickly send even a financially stable employee with good health insurance into a financial tailspin.

Employees face rising cost shares, higher deductibles, higher premiums, and rising out-of-pocket caps, meaning one rather typical medical event can cost them thousands they may not be prepared to pay. And if they face a more serious or disabling incident or illness, their ability or inability to cover out-of-pocket expenses and maintain viable income has immediate and long lasting financial implications for them and their loved ones. Compounding the problem is that most Americans, especially younger members of the workforce, think that something like a critical illness or disabling accident "is never going to happen to me."

After all, I personally know someone who fell, broke an arm, needed one ninety-minute surgery to install a metal plate and screws, had no complications, and yet her insurance was billed more than $130,000 before all was said and done. Yes, she had health insurance, solid emergency savings, and a good credit score. But she also had a high-deductible health plan and significant cost share. She still had to pay thousands out of pocket. She, in turn, knew someone diagnosed with throat cancer, and even though he had access to better-than-average medical benefits, rather than focusing 100 percent on his recovery and contributing part time on behalf of his employer, he spends his "good" days between chemo treatments reviewing the explanation of benefits (EOBs) and fighting with his doctor and insurance company. He's fighting a war on two fronts: for his life and for his livelihood, literally worried sick about the mountain of medical debt growing before his eyes.

"Your prescription is $30, but there's a $75 co-pay."

While the entire question of health insurance is not an easy one for employers, employees struggle with it as well. Can you blame them for being utterly stressed, mentally distracted, and wondering what else they or their employers could have done to help ease the blow of this one event? Can you imagine the financial and emotional consequences for someone without these advantages?

Can you imagine how they're second-guessing their decisions to turn down supplemental accident, critical illness, or medical indemnity insurance during the prior year's open enrollment? If only they'd better understood the real risks and the products themselves at the time of filling out those forms.

We all know of similar stories or have had similar experiences ourselves. These supplemental—and often overlooked or misunderstood—insurance policies play an important role in achieving financial fitness.

One reason it's easy for us to diminish the vast size and weight of this burden is because medical debt is a bit of a shapeshifter. It takes many forms. A person can rack it up when they use a credit card to cover a medical bill but don't pay it off or choose to prioritize a medical bill but then end up with a utility bill or car payment in collections.[1]

Accidents and illnesses happen all the time. That's why they're called "accidents" and not "never-ever" occurrences. It's impossible to know when they're going to happen and the severity of the situation. But what we can predict, sadly, is that they often affect our ability to continue to work and provide for ourselves and our families. This interruption, even when short-lived, can be damaging. In some cases, it can take a literal lifetime to dig out from under the debt one major medical event can generate.

Employers are trying to help, but measures vary widely. They offer solutions, but can do even more to combat this problem, helping their employees and themselves in the process.

Historical perspective

In the 1700s and 1800s, mutual-aid funds and doctor services were funded by deductions from workers' wages, often within a single company or trade association. This was frequently seen in higher-risk trades such as logging or mining. In fact, one of the largest modern regional health insurers in the U.S. was first founded as a cooperative to help meet the medical needs of logging workers in the Pacific Northwest.

BEHAVIOR NUDGES

Decision Paralysis

When given too many options, people tend to make the easiest decision, a poor decision, or no decision at all. This is one major reason employers should be very thoughtful about the benefits they offer and how they explain them to employees. Whether it's offering too many health plan options, too many random benefits, or too many investment options in a 401(k), employees tend to freeze up and do nothing when given too many choices.

In later decades, health and human welfare benefits were often at the center of workforce strikes.[2] After a series of rulings in favor of employees in the 1940s and 1950s, health insurance and other benefits became more and more commonplace.

Disability and coverages for illness began to appear in England around 1850 and, no pun intended, spread to the U.S. We could go on and on delving into the history, but the fact remains: these solutions eased some of the burden, but decades later the American marketplace still struggles with how to help workers and their families deal with the impact of illnesses and disabling events that remove workers from gainful employment for any meaningful period of time.

Fast-forward to 2011, and researchers such as Tal Gross and Matthew Notowidigbo found that out-of-pocket medical costs influenced 26 percent of bankruptcies in low-income households.

In 2015, the Kaiser Family Foundation found that medical bills led one million adults to declare bankruptcy. It also found that more than 25 percent of Americans age eighteen to sixty-four struggled to pay medical bills.

The challenge is as old as the employer-employee relationship is long.

The current landscape: the ever-increasing burden on employees

There has been some meaningful product innovation designed to help employees gain more control over the total cost of their health care. High-deductible health plans (HDHPs), paired with the tax-advantaged HSA (health savings account), have given both employers and employees an important new option. One that balances out-of-pocket costs, cost sharing, and employee/patient accountability for preventive care, maintaining their own health-care expenses insofar as they can control it, and making more informed decisions about how to use their health-care dollars.

Insurers and employers have started partnering to offer supplemental coverage options at very low cost relative to utility—hospital indemnity, accident, critical illness, and telemedicine—that employees can use *if* they understand them and *if* they can afford the added, incremental premiums. One of the major issues with all of these benefits is our decision-making behavior as humans. We like things that are simple and easy to understand, and we just don't do well when we have too many options. Too many options lead us to the very real trap of decision paralysis, and then we do nothing.

Despite this progress, even employees with access to seemingly "good" medical and disability benefits can be completely overwhelmed with medical expenses that aren't covered by their primary health insurance. And worker access to coverages and at-work benefits, along with their understanding of those coverages can—and do—vary wildly.

There is also a high cost and reputational risk for employers who don't take heed of the impact of health-care benefit decisions on employee safety. Most HR executives have heard the chilling stories, like the landmark 2011 case that cost one regional trucking company and their insurance partner a staggering $50 million legal judgment.

The company had transitioned to a high-deductible health plan (HDHP), with the family deductible set at the Accountable Care Act's allowed maximum. Under the plan, one of their drivers could no longer afford medications for several medical conditions. The driver's failing health and resulting fatigue caught up with him. He fell asleep at the wheel, resulting in a collision that killed him and a family of five. After fourteen months of negotiations, surviving family members were awarded a roughly $50 million financial settlement against the employer and insurance carrier. Obviously, the size and scope of those HDHPs has changed materially over the past decade, and those out-of-pocket premiums are now more in line with pre-HDHP options. But the example is still relevant, as people are often at a loss in terms of not knowing what they don't know in terms of predicting and managing health-care costs.

The infamous and tragic case was summarized countless times, including in a 2016 white paper from Innovu entitled, "The Future of Integrated Risk Management."

According to the white paper, "The presiding judge determined that the employer's decision to move to a high-deductible plan and the financial burden placed on its drivers (employees), in essence put its drivers and the American public in harm's way. The judge also ruled that the company was negligent in not fully understanding how its employees' health impacted their ability to safely perform their jobs. The judge found the company negligent because it did not fully understand the impact that cost-cutting health-care benefit decisions had on driver safety."

BEHAVIOR NUDGES

Pain of Paying

Some purchases or expenses are more painful than others, and people will try to avoid them despite big-picture considerations. For example, employees may delay getting vital medical care because they don't want the pain of paying initial deductibles.

Hugh O'Toole, Innovu's CEO and former President of Mass Mutual, is one of the leading industry disruptors when it comes to helping companies better understand why employers need to leverage data to connect health and financial wellness solutions in order to create better outcomes for employees, while simultaneously lowering costs and risk for the employer. O'Toole urges employers to keep the big picture in mind when considering health risks among their employee base and as they decide what benefits to offer. "Employers need to really think through implications of things like high-deductible health plans. For instance, if you have an employee base with a high rate of diabetes, it's very likely many of those employees will put off buying insulin or getting a vital test because it's too expensive. This will eventually backfire and lead to catastrophic claims that cost far more than the insulin or the test in the first place," he explains. "If employers can make good use of their data, and if they have strong consultants guiding them on their plan design, they can personalize plans, personalize guidance to employees, and buffer both the employee and the business from the ripple effect of extraordinary medical costs."

Again, there's no end to the dramatic anecdotes or scenarios that could be used to drive home the point that employees of all ages and income levels may struggle to cope with extraordinary medical expenses. The common thread within them all is that the outlook is grim for the majority of Americans when it comes to their ability to weather a major medical or disability event without incurring some form of debt.

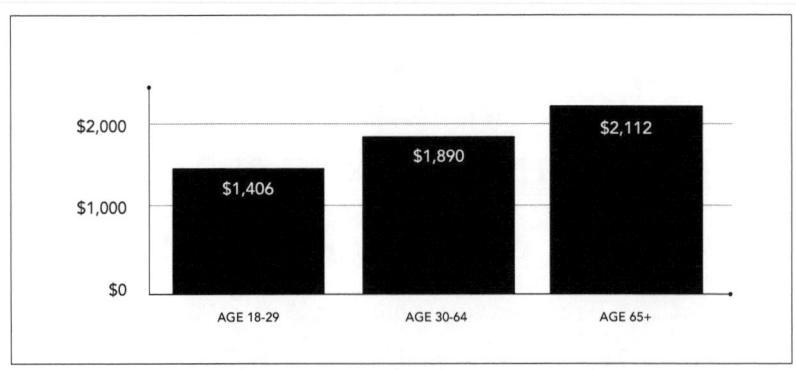

https://www.jpmorganchase.com/institute/research/healthcare/insight-coping-medical-payments

Within any given year, employees or retirees in every generation are likely to incur some sort of extraordinary medical expense. This is especially true as employees age, but regardless of age, expenses can erode financial wellness and create major stress.

And the pressure on employers to help solve the problem is only increasing, especially with aging Millennials and younger generations of workers, who look to the employer as a life and health coach. The rise of consumerism, increasing demand for transparency in pricing, and the uber-connectedness of workers within and beyond company walls is only making employees more informed and more demanding of employers. As financial pressures on employees grow, along with their access to information, the pressure employees exert on employers to offer solutions will also continue to build. The good news here is that the employer is increasingly up to the task of providing a safety net of solutions to its employees. Part parent, part ombudsman, part life coach, part therapist.

This problem—and the lack of cost transparency and real solutions—has been building for decades. And more recent public health crises like spikes in autism rates and the COVID-19 pandemic have forced health-related conversations to the forefront, driven legislative responses, and exerted maximum pressure on insurers and employers alike to respond. Now, more than ever, insurers and employers are under a hot and unforgiving spotlight to explain their medical benefits, expand offerings to cushion the blow of extraordinary medical expenses (including emotional and mental health-related expenses), and to be more transparent about who's paying for what and why.

The statistics

The statistics border on, well, sickening for anyone with a modicum of empathy or personal experience with costly health-related events.

- Roughly 137.1 million Americans faced financial hardship in 2019 because of medical costs.[3]

- Medical debt is the top reason that people, regardless of age, would consider cashing in their 401(k)s or other retirement savings.[4]

- It's estimated by multiple studies that 40–70 percent of personal bankruptcies are tied to medical debt, and of those filers, almost 80 percent of those who declared bankruptcy had health insurance.

- Almost a third of working Americans currently have some kind of medical debt and about 28 percent of those who have an outstanding balance owe $10,000 or more on their bills.[5]

- One in four U.S. workers risks becoming disabled before turning sixty-seven.

- Ninety-five percent of disabling accidents and illness are not work related and not covered by workers' comp.

- In 2018, the average Social Security Disability benefit was $1,233 monthly, while the 2019 federal poverty line for an individual was $1,012.

- Sixty-five percent of respondents surveyed say that most people need disability insurance. But the figure shrank to 48 percent when people were asked whether they believe they personally need it. The proportion shriveled to 20 percent when people were asked whether they actually have disability insurance.[6]

- One in five American workers acts as a caregiver for someone with special needs, such as an elder or special-needs child. (https://www.aarp.org/ppi/info-2020/caregiving-in-the-united-states).

- Sixty-eight percent of patients failed to fully pay off medical bill balances in 2016, up from 53 percent in 2015, and 49 percent in 2014. That percentage was projected to climb to 95 percent by 2020.[7]

- Medical bill collections tend to peak at about age twenty-seven and stay there through a person's mid-forties.[8]

- Americans spend more on health care than citizens of any other country, and that gap is projected to widen. Health-care spending is expected to consume almost 20 percent of the U.S. gross domestic product by 2027, according to a recent estimate from the Centers for Medicare & Medicaid Services.[9]

It's easy to see why this is one of the biggest hurdles preventing Americans—your employees—from achieving financial independence.

The challenge for employees

Let's look at the thin slice of disability for discussion purposes. Many employees, especially younger ones, don't think they'll ever get hurt at work. But the most common claims for disability insurance aren't on-the-job injuries. They're for illnesses, cancer, pregnancy, anxiety, and depression.

And if it does happen, these same younger employees may be poorly prepared to manage through it. It can take a dire toll on their financial and emotional wellness.

One moderately significant medical event—not even considered serious enough to trigger disability coverage—can leave employees stuck with payments for years as bills for copays and the "patient responsibility" portions pile up, one on top of the other.

These pressures are often compounded when employees are in a "sandwich" situation in which they're not only trying to care for themselves, they're also still raising children while at the same time trying to care for elderly or sick family members. The financial and emotional strain those employees face can be absolutely debilitating for them at times.

Any of these scenarios on a small scale can create a huge hurdle to employee financial wellness. Employees can be dumbstruck as they try to prioritize and juggle expenses. For instance, employees who are threatened by aggressive medical bill collectors may panic and divert money to cover those past-due bills rather than adding to their emergency savings, save for a down payment for a home, or contribute to retirement savings. This book is not meant to judge those individual decisions, as each person's situation is unique. But the fact is that a financial or consumer advisor might tell that person to take a breath and ignore the bill collector for the moment, even though that seems counterintuitive when you have someone on the phone threatening to destroy your credit. The point is that even the savviest employee may have absolutely no idea how to manage through a costly medical event. They may need to get expert help to know how to respond and which expenses to fund first. There are support systems in place to help individuals figure these sorts of things out, but they are not intuitive, easily accessible, and are oftentimes expensive. That is why the employer is the first place where employees are turning for guidance on these integrated health care and financial care decisions that are so interconnected.

What's worse, even extremely intelligent employees may not fully understand various coverages and therefore may be opting out at just the moment they may need them most.

If you polled employees or conducted focus groups, you may be shocked to find they don't understand various coverages and how they fit together to create the widest possible safety net. In fact, they may even view less-familiar coverages, such as hospital indemnity, as sketchy or gimmicky without fully understanding the legitimate purpose they serve. Or employees might purchase disability coverage without fully realizing that, frankly, it contains so many restrictions and vague definitions that it can be virtually useless at the moment they need it most.

When I sit down with even the most senior management teams, many don't realize that their disability coverage replaces only 10–20 percent, or less, of their total compensation. That's a real eye-opener and conversation starter. And this is coming from the people putting these plans in place. If they don't understand what they actually have, how can you expect your employees to?

Opportunities for employers

This massive burden of medical debt on the American worker can be viewed as an opportunity for employers. Those who offer more complete solutions and educate their employee base on how and why to take advantage of them will be the best poised to attract and retain the best and brightest workforce of the future.

Use this prompt to be ready for an inevitably shifting labor market with an attractive, meaningful, curated mix of health-related benefits. At the time of this writing, the economy and the employee have been dealt an incredibly hard blow by COVID-19. But when the market shifts back to favor the job seeker, you'll be ready, because employees are going to move toward employers who responded in meaningful ways to the greatest public health crisis of our time. This could mean revisiting your voluntary benefits. "Something like critical illness or accident insurance, or hospital indemnity, is a more finely tuned, efficient insurance vehicle, so that it allows people to target what would give them the best peace of mind at the lowest price," says Jeff Faber, Chief Strategy Officer at HUB International. He also foresees the most innovative employers offering customized selections for someone who's twenty-six and starting a family or someone who's fifty-six and preparing to retire.

Make every effort possible to help employees create a bigger, stronger safety net against the extraordinary medical expenses that add to their personal debt load. Even if you can only offer it on a voluntary basis, try to add benefits like extended voluntary disability coverage (to help them replace more income), critical illness, and hospital indemnity coverages. The return they offer, relative to their cost to you and your employee, can be enormous.

Amp up your employee education efforts. This is important across all demographics, but especially with younger employees. Educating a younger consumer on the merits of critical illness insurance or disability coverage, and convincing them that it's worth paying a premium to cover an event they don't see happening to them, is a tough hill to climb. But with some added focus on crystal-clear, concrete communication around how various benefits work together to create a safety net, it can be done. This will take an omni-channel approach that may even call for not only digital engagement tools but also some good old-fashioned small-group meetings (in-person or virtual), and maybe even some incentive to get them to participate. It also means thinking outside the box on your benefits communications. For example, have you done enough to help employees understand how various coverages fit together? Do your enrollment communications help employees look beyond the basics of premiums and deductibles to think in terms of total value? If they don't, they need some attention.

Look at your medical benefits through the lens of conscious capitalism and corporate social responsibility. Do they really measure up? If you think they do, would your employees, job candidates, and activist shareholders agree? Virtually any employer that wants to compete in hiring a high-performing workforce in this modern era (in which businesses are also expected to be good corporate citizens) needs to take an intellectually honest look at whether it's doing all it can to help employees understand, anticipate, and insure against extraordinary medical expenses—as well as dealing with debilitating medical debt—and the often-broader implications that may exist for your business and your brand reputation.

If you've counted on your employees not knowing any better, think again. Changing demographics and behaviors, fueled further by COVID, have prompted employees in all demographics to become much more deeply engaged in understanding their workplace benefits. They're comparing notes and casting a skeptical eye at employers who offer what they view as meager health-related benefits.

Lean on consultants and providers. Work with your advisors and health and medical insurance partners to expand your education efforts. You can have a real, positive impact on employees by ensuring they understand the purpose and mechanics of various types of coverage. This can show up for employees in big and small ways. For example, are your open enrollment materials full of provider-generated content that's full of jargon? Take a stand on behalf of employees and make sure your materials are written in the clearest, most direct language. This can ultimately serve you and the employee in the long run. Or take, for instance, surprise medical bills. Employees are often caught flatfooted and don't know how to respond to them. But they have a profound impact on employee stress levels, financial stability, and the ability to focus on their work. Be proactive in finding ways to educate employees before the unexpected occurs, so they can be more prepared.

Future outlook

Companies will have to examine their ethics, financials, culture, and their existing and future workforce to determine what their health and medical benefits lineup should be.

It's also critical to bear in mind that financial education changes behavior in only one in a thousand people. It takes a clear, loud, and steady drumbeat to have real impact. This will take ingenuity from employers, who will have to think outside the box. Think back to your second-grade self, where, according to the *Harvard Business Review*, 96 percent of us thought of ourselves as creative. Don't resort back to the graduating senior from high school, where only 6 percent thought of ourselves as creative. And yes, this is a slight indictment of our educational system, which can sometimes zap the creativity out of learning. That said, employers know what is needed, we have the solutions, and we need to creatively think of ways to help employees see the light.

Some legislative relief may eventually come to fruition for consumers. At the time of this writing, bipartisan legislation is currently being examined to protect individuals from surprise out-of-network medical bills. But beyond insuring to the hilt through employer-sponsored coverage and the coverage they might piece together for themselves, employees really get very little legislative air cover.

Additionally, we may start to see more "nudge" solutions in the form of default enrollment of employees in a mix of coverages in order to help control collective cost and risk for employers, employees, and insurers alike. After all, how did we "nudge" people to purchase auto insurance? It became a legal condition for getting a driver's license. How did the 401(k) explode in prevalence? From default enrollment that leapfrogged right over employee inertia or lack of knowledge. Prescriptive moves like this can reduce confusion for consumers and protect them from their own poor decision-making or lack of understanding.

The more you can do to help employees develop a financial road map that includes a readiness plan for responding to extraordinary medical expenses over the short and long term, the more you'll benefit in the long run with healthier, more stable, more focused, more present, less absent employees. At the end of the day, this all points back not just to your offering mix, but to the need for broad financial literacy and planning. If you can offer education and proactive strategies beyond just helping your employees choose plan A, B, or

C during open enrollment, you can help them overcome one of the greatest modern financial impediments and keep them moving forward on the road to overall financial wellness.

Questions to consider

- Do our managers and employees know that extraordinary medical expenses are the leading cause of bankruptcy in the U.S.?

- Are we offering the right mix of voluntary benefits that provide employees with the best possible safety net for managing health-care expenses not covered by our health plan?

- Are we showcasing our voluntary health/medical and disability benefits in a way that employees can easily understand them and how they complement each other?

- For any employee, including executives, do we truly understand our disability coverage and exactly what it provides?

- If we have low uptake on voluntary benefits such as critical illness or hospital indemnity, do we know why employees are not enrolling?

- How are we prioritizing our total benefits spend between health and financial wellness and are we considering them together as part of a holistic strategy?

5

HOUSING EXPENSES: WAKING UP FROM THE AMERICAN DREAM

"The cost of living hasn't affected its popularity."

—Mark Twain, American author

While housing expenses are not the biggest obstacle standing between American workers and financial wellness, they're still worth examining for the financial stress they can create. After all, our decisions about housing and where we choose to call home are among the most intensely personal, most impactful choices any of us will make over a lifetime. Where we live has some effect not only on our financial wellness, but an enormous impact on our overall happiness and well-being. It's where we laugh, cry, sleep, eat, and seek refuge. During the 2020 COVID pandemic, it's where we nested and where many of us have spent the bulk of our disposable income (if we had any to spare) during the ensuing shutdown.

But it's an incredibly complicated topic. We can be irrational, confused, and emotional as we try to make sound decisions about housing—especially regarding home ownership. Why is that? There are four big reasons:

1. **Generations of Americans have been all but brainwashed to believe that home ownership is the very pinnacle of the American dream.** Think about it: when else could you convince most reasonable people to take out a loan of $200,000 or more, pay several hundred thousand more in interest expense, and think it was a good idea? Nowhere else would we consider such a horrible proposition except when it comes to home ownership.

2. **Follow the money.** The government made mortgage interest expense tax deductible, so of course people are going to take the bait on that, while forgetting they're biting a hook in the form of a mortgage they'll be stuck with for fifteen or thirty years.

3. **We got lulled into viewing homes as perpetually appreciating assets.** That is until the housing bubble burst and countless Americans ended up upside down as their home values plummeted. For a long time, we just weren't doing the math on things like the total interest expense. But that seems to be changing.

4. **It's ridiculously easy to forget about the total cost of home ownership.** We end up so focused on the mortgage that we often forget about the insurance, upkeep, utilities, etc. that will also demand a sizable portion of our monthly cash flow. We also are constantly tempted to spend money on things like furniture, décor, and "improvements" like fancy new decks or outdoor kitchens because we can convince ourselves they're assets. But rarely do we ever recover one-hundred cents on the dollar for any of those upgrades. And the bigger the house, the bigger the trap. It's sort of like having a big pocketbook or a big closet: you'll just keep filling it up if you're not careful. And trust me, I can be just as prone to this type of thinking as the next guy or gal.

It took us a while to wake up to these realities. But things are changing rapidly, especially among Millennials and younger age groups. For Baby Boomers and older Gen Xers, home ownership embodied the American Dream. For some, however, home ownership is simply no longer a priority or an option. They may dream of owning a home, but they may be so strapped with debt that this part of the American Dream is slipping away while they drown in student loan debt and ever-expanding credit card balances. Or they may see home ownership as a weight, a burden, and something that might divert money and time from experiences they'd rather enjoy with their time, resources, and YOLO-meets-FOMO mentalities.

Regardless of personal opinions about the virtues or vices of home ownership, leasing, renting, home equity loans, or other modes of paying for housing, it's critically important for employers to consider the impact of housing costs and the related anxieties on employee financial wellness. Employees can be completely confused about how to prioritize cash flow. Should they pay down their credit cards rather than saving for a down payment? Should they fix the roof or make an extra payment on their student loan? It can be an incredibly difficult juggling act, especially for employees who carry debt and don't have a clear financial plan.

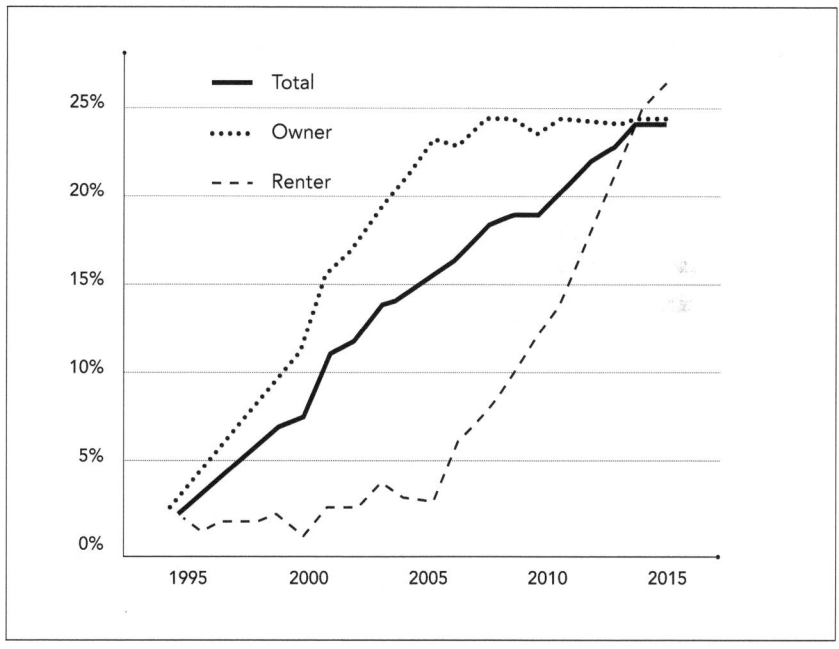

https://www.zillow.com/research/renter-owner-household-growth-8666/)

There will continue to be periods such as this run that started in 2005, in which the number of renter households began climbing and surpassed the number of owner households. That's in part because home ownership has lost its luster for younger generations, many of whom see home ownership as a dead weight versus a dream.

More often than we may realize, that little black cloud over our heads, following us no matter where we go, has a lot of pent-up housing-related precipitation in it. You know the adage: "House rich, cash poor." That's in large part because it can be very easy to overlook the total cost of home ownership, from property taxes to insurance to utilities to lawn care to furnishings to planned and unplanned maintenance costs.

Additionally, current and prospective homeowners alike can underestimate the risk of having so much money tied up in a single asset. The calamities of foreclosures and bankruptcies that can result from having all your eggs in one basket were front-page news during the Great Recession a mere decade ago. That moment in time reminded us that we can not only be overexposed in a single stock, but that we can also be overexposed by being invested in a home we thought would always appreciate. Consumers took the hard lesson well at the time, but how quickly we forget.

Historical perspective

Humans and our relationship with the idea of "home" and home ownership have been evolving for thousands of years. For early man, home was impermanent and often portable. It had to enable access to food sources, which often meant following herds of animals to hunt or finding water sources. Once we learned how to tame, cultivate, and store the precious resources, we were able to put down roots. The Bible and other religious and philosophical texts extoll the virtues of home. Countless artists and singers, from Michael Bublé to Dierks Bentley to Edward Sharp and the Magnetic Zeros, express the notion of "home" as a symbol of peace and love.

In the modern era, especially in America where land has generally been plentiful, owning a home became central to the American Dream. Generations from pioneers to Baby Boomers to Gen Xers and even Millennials have pursued home ownership, often urged by our parents and others to uphold the dream and to buy a home as both a sound investment and a badge that we had "arrived" as responsible adults.

For decades, the biggest piece of debt many of us held was a mortgage, and it was socially acceptable. After all, we were funding a reliably appreciating asset . . . right? For decades, that was generally true. After all, who cared if you had hundreds of thousands of dollars of debt? It's not real debt anyway; it's just a mortgage, right?!

Back in the day, barring local or short-term blips here and there, consumers could generally count on their homes to be pretty good investments. The American Dream was wrapped up in a white picket fence, a lawnmower, maybe a porch swing, and ghastly avocado or almond-colored kitchen appliances. We didn't need to save 10–15 percent of our paycheck for retirement, as we were all covered by our pension plans. We decided to send a man to the moon. We had grand hopes. The three TV networks were full of programming that featured families—in freestanding suburban homes—that

BEHAVIOR NUDGES

Sunk Cost Effect

Once we invest in a particular path, our commitment to it grows whether it's wise or not. This can cause us to make a string of bad decisions or to "throw good money after bad money." For example, we may continue sinking money into an aging home, when the best decision for us may actually be to rent or downsize to a smaller, newer home.

---

examined and extolled some version of family values. And owning a home was core to those values.

The government encouraged home ownership by making the interest on mortgages tax deductible beginning in 1913. That said, the impact and importance of that tax deductibility didn't really come into play until after WWII, the expansion of transportation, and the open development of suburbia, coupled with broad-based updates to the tax code. This little nudge did wonders for the explosion of home ownership in this country and in furthering the idyllic American Dream. After all, a tax incentive is one of the most effective nudges when it comes to humans and money. Every presidential administration has espoused the virtues of home ownership because it was

Then and now

My parents, who came to this country with nothing more than a small wooden basket of clothes, recall that their first house purchase in Evansville, Indiana, was possible because everyone told them that was what they should do, including the government and the local bank. They actually borrowed the money for the 10 percent down payment. That's right, it was 100 percent financed. They were two kids in their twenties doing what they thought was right. It didn't make good sense then, and it might not make the best sense now.

good for the economy. But they forgot to teach us how to assess whether home ownership really made good sense over time.

There was even what I think of as quiet "rent shaming" among Gen Xers as we were coming of age and into our late twenties. Many who did choose to buy homes—current writer excluded—often looked down haughtily on renters, secretly wondering what was wrong with our friends who chose to keep renting rather than buying when we hit our late twenties. After all, could they not pull together or borrow enough for a modest down payment? Was their credit bad? But then 2008–2010 came along, and a giant housing bubble exploded in our faces. Many were left stunned and confused as home values plummeted and thousands lost their homes or had their credit destroyed.

While interest on a mortgage is still tax deductible, interest on home equity loans is no longer tax deductible as of 2018. It's interesting that home equity lines of credit (HELOCs) were quite the thing for the Gen-X crowd. It was added to the mortgage as an additional tax-deductible line of credit, like a seemingly limitless low-interest credit card that was originally intended for household improvements. (Pretty sure that went out the window, as I was using it for Costco runs and concert tickets. I can only imagine the crafty folks who came up with this idea, sitting around the mahogany boardroom table thinking, "Yep, this is a definitely a good idea; I can't see anything that could go wrong with this." We've mentioned before that virtually no one in this country has had any financial literacy training, right?) For many, these HELOCs simply turned homes into ATMs for things like cars and vacations that would do nothing to sustain or increase a home's value. And they only compounded the severity of the recession for those who'd taken out home equity loans thinking their homes would never depreciate, and they'd have no trouble essentially servicing two home loans.

Young Millennials, then aged eighteen to twenty-eight, had a front-row seat to the devastation and family displacement. They saw that the most sacred asset, your home, could be taken away or become the center of household financial distress. For all of us who were adults at the time, but especially for Millennials, their sense of "home" and its permanence was dismantled and recast. They also were entering the job market at a time when wage increases came to a screeching halt. And as noted above, most adults have weathered at least one housing bubble burst and knew at least one person who was forced into a short sale. Millennials in particular have a real anxiety when it comes to financial security, with a view of "home" as fluid—and it's no wonder.

The current landscape

In a relatively short time, so much has changed in the world in terms of lifestyle preferences and the housing industry. A quick online search of "renting versus buying" returns countless articles with headlines like, "Buying a home has long been considered the American dream. But is home ownership a good investment? Or, much like a fancy sports car, is it just a status symbol?"[1]

Millennials have overwhelmingly been renters. In the finance world, we've

© Glasbergen/ glasbergen.com

"Enjoy your new home, Cinderella, but remember —
at midnight your mortgage turns into a heavy boulder
that you have to carry for the next 30 years!"

talked for a decade of their lack of spending on capital goods. (Homes, washers, dryers, cars—you know, "expensive" things.)

Housing costs are another huge factor in the decision to rent or buy. They've been rising rapidly in many of the most desirable geographies, as gentrification is shaping cities and who can afford to live where. The opposite is true for many cities in the North (namely those centered around obsolete or hobbling industries), which have seen inflation-adjusted, stagnant home prices now for decades. Meantime, debt levels have been rising, while movements like material and financial minimalism have taken hold.

Additionally, technology has made us more mobile. The gig workforce is expanding rapidly and, with that, remote work models. If we look to where the Millennial mobile workforce is moving—cities like Nashville, Charlotte, Denver, and Austin, with strong job markets and attractive lifestyles—we see cranes hovering over new apartment buildings as far as the eye can see.

According to "America's Rental Housing 2020," a study from the Joint Center for Housing Studies of Harvard, "New rental construction remains near its highest levels in three decades. Despite the slowdown in demand, multifamily starts rose 6 percent in 2018 to 374,100 units—the third-highest total since the late 1980s. Production in 2019 is set to match or even exceed that number."

The migration has transformed these once-smaller cities into bustling and vibrant magnets for an array of professionals and Millennials alike. My friend Matt Wiltshire, as the Head of Economic Development for Nashville over the past decade and an advocate for public transportation, has seen the explosive growth, commercialization, tourism, and sophistication of the arts and commerce that has attracted hordes of people from Seattle, Los Angeles, Chicago, and New York. Matt says, "A favorite pastime for those who live in or frequent Nashville, Tennessee (also known to many as Music City or "Nashvegas") is to count the number of cranes hovering over midtown, the dynamic and trendy Gulch redevelopment zone, and downtown."

It's also interesting to see the metropolitan housing or city planning initiatives that were set in motion in urban areas nationwide over the past few decades. Countless development and redevelopment projects feature the integration of work, living, and shopping together in the same areas, in proximity to public transportation where possible. This reflects so many aspects of our changing culture and demographics. Urban planners can only hope the flight to the suburbs and exurbs in response to COVID-19 is temporary. But if we take the long view, we may see it as just a blip in the decades-long shift in urban planning and zoning that has crisscrossed this country in anticipation of a population of 500 million Americans by the end of the century.[2]

Consumers took the lessons from the Great Recession and now better understand the reality that they could end up in an area or moment in time where property values are going down and taxes are going up. Chicago anyone? And "black-swan" events like the COVID-19 pandemic have forced us to confront the reality that being locked into home ownership can drastically affect how nimble we can be in responding to a crisis. We're finally taking a slightly broader view and stepping more cautiously into the massive commitment of home ownership.

The fintech industry is also seeing the need for housing comparison tools and stepping in with solutions. Companies like Own Up claim to help consumers compare mortgages and lenders for free. One of their taglines is, "We built Own Up to bring clarity to an outdated industry." But even they get compensated by lenders.

Another fintech firm, EarnUp, offers a mortgage payment management system. Kristen Berman, Cofounder of Irrational Labs together with Dan Ariely, Professor of Economics, Duke University, highlights this as an example of a specific solution employers could integrate with payroll. "Employees split their mortgage payment into two monthly payments. What's great is that 64 percent of people choose to pay more than required by the lender, and ultimately make five additional payments each year. It can save them thousands of dollars and significantly shorten the life of a loan," she explains.

All of this boils down to one big shift: our thinking about home ownership as a priority is beginning to change in ways we might not have predicted. While we still have huge blind spots in our ability to make sound housing decisions, we are starting to view home ownership with a more discerning eye.

Sure, people still want to be in nice, safe neighborhoods with good access and good schools, but even those with children are renting more and more. Whereas home ownership may have been the centerpiece of a personal financial strategy in the 1950s through the 1990s, that's just not the case anymore.

Add to all this the fact that we're becoming a nation of subscribers. From streaming entertainment with Netflix, to data storage, to meal kit delivery, to food delivery from GrubHub, to our borrowed or subscription wardrobes from TrunkClub, StitchFix, and Rent the Runway, we want flexibility and convenience with few or no strings attached. This mind shift toward a subscription mode is infiltrating our views on housing. Renting has become "du jour" for Millennials.

Home ownership was once a no-brainer as a financial priority, a foundational building block for financial stability and reliable value play. But taking all these emerging factors together, it's not so clear-cut anymore.

The statistics

One could get lost in the sea of available housing-related data. And it's not always clear-cut. But what employers should take from it is that preferences for home ownership are generally falling in favor of renting among their younger employees. And yet, for those who may want to own a home, the debt burdens they're facing (e.g., student loans and credit cards) is making it tough for them to save for down payments, juggle cash flow, and afford the total cost of owning a home.

- The average growth rate of home values in the U.S. since 1890 is only 3.2 percent.[3]

- It takes roughly five years or more to break even on a traditional fixed-rate mortgage.

- On average, Millennials move about every two years, compared to Boomers, who say they typically have moved every six years.[4]

- Millennials need to put away about 15 percent more than previous generations to afford a home,[5] because their salaries have not kept pace with rising home prices.

- Only 13 percent of Millennial renters across the U.S. will be able to afford a traditional 20 percent down payment within the next five years.[6]

- Just over 12 percent of Millennial renters plan to "always" rent.[7]

- In some U.S. markets, it can take a decade or more for a home buyer with an average income to save for a 20 percent down payment.[8]

The challenge for employees

Some employees may have total clarity that home ownership is not for them. Others may want to buy but may be so busy servicing debt such as credit cards and student loans, they can't pull together money for a down payment.

Or they may be house poor, with so much money tied up in a mortgage, utilities, rising property taxes, revolving credit lines on the furniture, and hundreds of dollars in maintenance expenses. Even if they're lucky enough to be in an area with rising home values, it doesn't mean they've made housing choices that are actually contributing to their overall financial wellness.

Others may have banks more than willing to give them mortgage loans with only 5 percent down. (It doesn't mean they should take it. If their house depreciates, they could end up upside down and their equity could be wiped out.) Consumers need to account for numerous factors, like local home prices, rental rates, wage patterns, the regional economy, where they may be living over the next several years, and the structure of loans. Each person's situation is unique and needs to be assessed on the above factors, not to mention their total debt load, income potential, job stability, health-care costs, education costs, and more. The math is complicated and subtle, and it can stump even seasoned financial experts.

With the best intentions, employees may be making some very miscalculated, emotion-driven decisions about housing without even knowing it. They need help viewing their housing decisions with the same analytical eye one would and should apply to investing in stocks. Employees need help looking at the full picture—including risk assessment—when it comes to the very critical decision of how to spend their housing dollars.

Opportunities for employers

While employers haven't historically been very engaged in this aspect of employee financial well-being, some employers are seeing that employees may need help in making sound housing-related decisions. For those employers that do want to try to help, MetLife suggests basic benefits that could be offered to employees, such as these:[9]

- Prepaid legal plans that can help employees manage closing costs and get support in negotiating housing-related contracts

- Credit union relationships

- Group rates on homeowners insurance

The National Housing Conference also cites down payment assistance, home buyer education, and rental search assistance as examples of employer-assisted housing, which they define as any housing rental or ownership program that is "financed or assisted by any employer."[10]

And it's not only the employee who benefits from employer-sponsored support and resources. The Fels Institute of Government at the University of Pennsylvania points out that employer-assisted programs can also benefit employers. In a 2018 piece, they point out that, "As workers are forced to live farther from their workplace, their productivity declines." Granted, this was before the era of COVID, before millions of workers were suddenly forced into remote work. While COVID will leave a permanent imprint on society and ways of working, this time-tested connection between things like housing location, commute time, and work productivity are sure to still hold true at some level as the world returns to an in-person work model. After all, manufacturing, production, logistics, hospitality, and other collaborative industries are not going away.

What does it all mean? While humans will always need shelter, our preferences in housing will evolve and change as society evolves and changes. The greatest assistance an employer can offer is to provide tools and services that help employees become more financially literate and get expert help developing detailed financial plans that examine their housing decisions as part of an overall financial strategy.

Heather Holmes, Founder and CEO of fintech and AI-driven financial planning company Genivity, echoes the sentiment about the employer as the most logical source of broad financial education. She says, "Employers are uniquely positioned to provide education to their employees. And it's in the employer's best interest to fill the void. The outcome can be a more stable, more thriving employee environment."

Anything employers can offer to help employees sift through the competing priorities of retirement, credit card debt servicing, emergency savings, daycare, education, auto, health-care costs, and more will help employees make better decisions when it comes to housing. For many, these things may simply take much higher precedence than a mortgage. But maybe not.

There are vendor partners out there. But as with any benefit offering, employers should be discerning with the partners they choose if they want to be a true advocate for employees. For example, fintech vendor SoFi advertises on the vendor directory of the Society for Human Resource Management (SHRM) as a mortgage loan and refinancing provider. Their summary states, "It's harder than ever for your employees trying to buy their first home, particularly in urban areas with high prices and 20 percent down payment requirements— SoFi's unique underwriting approach allows borrowers to qualify for more financing than traditional lenders offer." While that may sound fantastic on its face, borrowing more may be the last temptation an employee needs.

More than anything, the question of housing expenses points us back to the broader need for financial planning. Experts like Charles Whelan, Senior Lecturer of Public Policy and Economics at Dartmouth College, and author of *The New York Times* bestseller, *Naked Economics*, agree. He says, "We hear all this public discourse on student debt, health-care costs, and housing. We have to go back to basic financial planning. It's all about reframing. Having the basic skills necessary to do the basic math, including the math on how to spend your housing dollar, is the essence of personal finance and financial wellness."

What does the future hold?

While nobody has a crystal ball, it's evident that our societal views on housing are shifting in some very significant and possibly lasting ways. Prior to COVID, we were seeing many consumers—especially Millennials—opting to rent rather than buy, and gravitating toward city centers, walkable cities, mixed-use developments, areas with robust public transportation, and the like. That makes perfect sense as we evolve toward a subscription-based, on-demand society, and a society that generally places an increasing premium on experiences and work-life balance.

We are also seeing influences of minimalism, environmentalism, and the ideal of the mobile, unencumbered citizen showing up in movements like the tiny house craze.

Just as the rest of our lives are shifting to a subscription (i.e., rental) model, younger generations are growing up viewing housing as something more fluid and less permanent than prior generations. They want to be able to change or turn off and on their housing selections at will—and may not want to be too tied down.

But as is always the case with humans and economics, the wind changes direction frequently. As the COVID pandemic unfolded, people became much more interested in space, in land, and in getting out of densely populated cities and into the suburbs, exurbs, and rural areas. The future remains to be seen, and this could turn out to be a temporary blip.

But regardless of the trend du jour or momentary disruptions to the housing market, it's important for employers to keep a pulse on what's happening with housing in general, so you can understand how it may be affecting the financial well-being of your employees. After all, housing costs (along with student loan debt) eat up the greatest portion of the American paycheck. So whether your employees rent or purchase, housing costs—for the foreseeable future—will remain one of the greatest financial pressures your employees face over the course of their careers.

Questions to consider

- Are we fully aware of housing costs in the areas where our employees work and live, as well as the total impact of those costs on their financial wellness?

- Do we have any credit union, mortgage comparison tools, or other vendors or partners that can help employees better understand and manage housing costs?

- Are we offering employees basic tools and education to help them assess and manage their housing-related costs more effectively?

PART III—MEGATRENDS

Over the next decade, six megatrends will have a profound influence on workplace financial wellness programs and on the value exchange between employers and employees. On the benefits plan design side, these trends will push employers to think more broadly and more innovatively about the needs of employees, especially their personal financial needs. On the employee side, these trends will continue to have profound impacts on their behaviors, needs, preferences, and their influence on employers.

In part, I chose to explore these trends for the outsized impact they are already having on the employer-employee relationship and on the workplace benefits industry. I believe these trends will only continue to grow in importance. In that regard, they should be issues that every member of your benefits team is aware of and understands the role each trend might have in how you choose and deliver your employee benefits. These trends will surely force employers of all sizes, in all industries, to respond with benefits that create better financial, health, and life outcomes for employees and support a workforce that's healthy, focused, and able to perform optimally. I know, because as an expert who talks with employers and employees, day in and day out, I see the influence these trends are having and will continue to have.

The emergence of these trends is being driven by dramatic, primarily demographic realignment in the United States. This includes the sheer number of Millennials replacing Baby Boomers as the drivers of public policy and the economy, and the precarious state of personal financial wellness in the U.S., under which more than 75 percent of Americans report that they live with daily financial anxiety.[1]

While certainly important enough on an individual basis, it is the confluence of these six trends that is now setting the precedence for unparalleled advancements in workplace financial wellness. When we look at them in their entirety is when we truly begin to see the full picture of transformation, and the urgency and opportunity behind it.

Employers that heed these key trends, and actively look for concrete ways to factor them into their benefits planning as part of a thoughtful human capital strategy, will be the employers in the very best position to attract, hire, and retain the workforce of the future.

6

SHIFTING DEMOGRAPHICS: THE CHANGING FACE OF THE AMERICAN EMPLOYEE

"If the statistics are boring, then you've got the wrong numbers."

—Edward Tufte, American statistician

Just as the most successful consumer and B2B brands pay close attention to customer demographics, successful employers pay close attention to ever-changing workforce demographics as well.

As businesspeople, we know that demographics matter. It's one of the first things we learn in business school. Sure, demographics might seem boring at times. But they hold important keys. They tell us stories and reveal patterns. They give us a manageable way to divide humans into cohorts and make more informed business decisions about what they need and what products and services we should offer them.

By making sure you're fully tuned in to your employee census and what the underlying demographics tell you, you can get a solid grip on what your employees may be grappling with financially, and what they need and expect from you as an employer. And demographics will help you form a more complete picture of your workforce and their spoken and unspoken needs. This, in turn, can help you ask the right questions and make sure the benefits you're offering are targeted and meaningful to both current and future employees.

For instance, Millennials have overtaken Boomers as the largest population segment in the U.S. As the Boomer generation rolls away from the workforce, Millennials are now approximately 100 million strong and will make up more than three-fourths of the voting and working public by 2025. Their size, scale, and diversity of thought are driving public policy and the rapid evolution of workplace wellness solutions. Millennials are shouldering $1.7 trillion of student loan debt, not to mention credit card debt, housing and childcare expenses, and other serious burdens. They grew up with helicopter parents and saw the devastation of the Great Recession on their parents and grandparents. It's enough to give anyone migraines, or worse.

Given the stats and what we know about behaviors and preferences of Millennials (first-generation digital natives who understandably expect seamless online experiences in every area of their lives), it's no wonder they shoulder anxieties—they're stressed out about money and expect employers to provide more of a financial road map for them, well beyond what previous generations expected. As Brian Graff, CEO of The American Retirement Association explains it, "Millennials have more of a need for handholding and shepherding, to put it in very general terms. I see that as a manager now. I've had to approach management differently because of how Millennials grew up. It's reflected in everything. They want and need employers to help them cope with their lives, which is a complete cultural change from thirty to forty years ago."

It's time for us to use what we know about their unique reality to start giving them meaningful support.

And depending on your industry and the composition of your workforce, Millennials aren't your only consideration. You surely have at least some number of Gen Xers, incoming Gen Zers (a.k.a. Zoomers) and maybe a healthy number of Boomers as well. They each have their own needs and struggles when it comes to managing their finances.

A study of demographics can point you and your teams in the right direction and help you form solid hypotheses about which financial benefits mean the most to your employees. By having a sense of who they are at a group and individual level, you can improve your ability to hire and retain the employees you need, while also helping to improve their financial wellness. You can also make sure your benefits strategy is both tailored and targeted so that you can focus business resources on offering and supporting the most important benefits in the most efficient way possible. And again, a financially healthier, less-anxious employee is infinitely more productive, happier, and present.

The big picture: current demographic "buckets"

First, let's make sure we're aligned on terms. After all, it can be challenging, at best, to remember who belongs in which group. I'm a Gen Xer and half the time I can't even remember exactly how old I am, let alone how we're defined. By first anchoring in each of the major demographic segments (when they were born, how old they are, and remembering just how many of them there are), you can ensure you and your teams are on the same page when discussing these key groups.

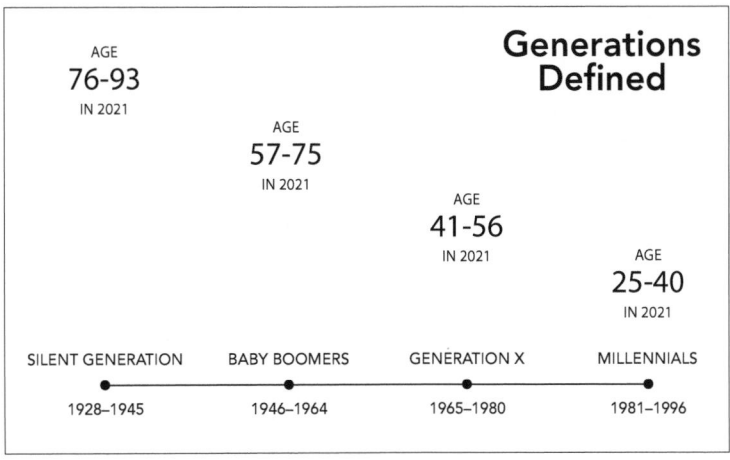

General financial wellness: who's dealing with what when it comes to managing personal finances

Each generation naturally has an array of financial obligations and is wrestling with financial anxiety at some level. It doesn't matter if you are twenty-two or seventy-two, surely you either are currently or have had the little black cloud of financial stress following overhead at all times of the day. Admit it, it has cast a dark shadow on your parade more than once—when you've been in a meeting at the office, on a Zoom call with a client, or hosting a BBQ in the backyard. It's omnipresent, and it impacts us in ways we are only now beginning to understand and manage. While no two individuals are alike, it can be eye-opening to examine and look across each of the major demographic groups and see what's happening with them at a high level.

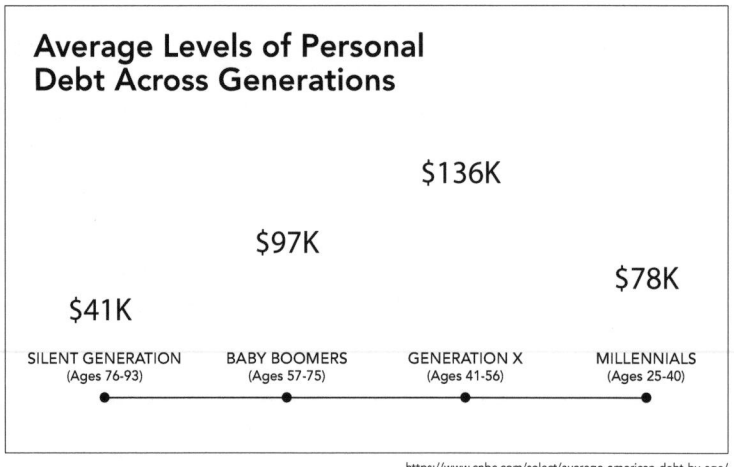

Average Levels of Personal Debt Across Generations

$136K

$97K

$78K

$41K

| SILENT GENERATION | BABY BOOMERS | GENERATION X | MILLENNIALS |
| (Ages 76-93) | (Ages 57-75) | (Ages 41-56) | (Ages 25-40) |

https://www.cnbc.com/select/average-american-debt-by-age/

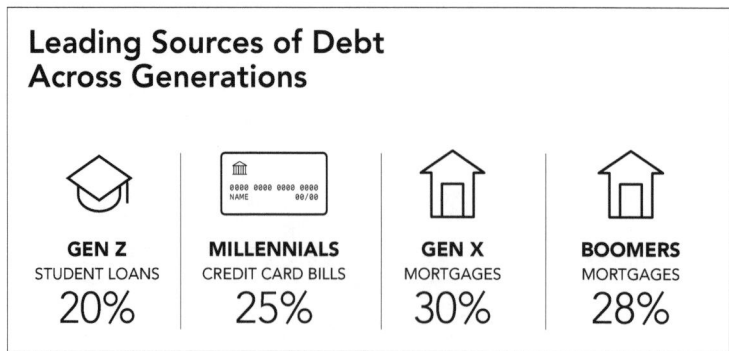

Leading Sources of Debt Across Generations

GEN Z	MILLENNIALS	GEN X	BOOMERS
STUDENT LOANS	CREDIT CARD BILLS	MORTGAGES	MORTGAGES
20%	25%	30%	28%

The Baby Boomers: ready to retire, but not always necessarily with confidence

Born: 1946–1964

Current age: 56–74

Where they need help: Retiring with confidence and understanding how they are going to turn that savings nest egg into a retirement income stream on which they are going to be able to live for ten, twenty, thirty, or forty years. Retirement income planning is perhaps the most important and complicated aspect of financial wellness, and yet still one of the most difficult to understand. In addition, as Boomers transition to that next part of their life journey, it comes with a heavy weight of apprehension, uncertainty, and anxiety over what they'll do in the coming years. And how will they define themselves if they are no longer working? This is one of those seminal moments in life—life becomes much more clearly focused, seen in more finite terms. For Boomers, it's scary to take the polar plunge into retirement.

This generation earned its name due to the significant increase in birth rates following World War II. Soldiers returned home from war, society was jubilant over the Allied victory, and people had more time and resources to start families. Baby Boomers grew up in an era of suburban development, increasing U.S. influence, advances in science and technology, and the pursuit and the realization of the American Dream.

Many observers say that their shared positive childhood experiences may be why Baby Boomers tend to be optimistic, individualistic, and worked so hard to attain the American Dream. This generation has generally tended to value interpersonal relationships because they did not grow up with technology, which tends to extend relationships beyond your local communities. They tend to be career-focused, competitive individuals who strive for jobs that provide them with wealth and recognition.

Boomers have a wealth of subject-matter expertise, and tons of experience dealing with people. They have enormous intellectual capital, and the tribal knowledge that comes from long tenures with their employers. They may be aging out but dismissing them means you risk losing an enormous amount of organizational wisdom—all the subtle cultural knowledge and organizational quirks that don't fit into a spreadsheet or a cheery new employee orientation session. They came of age in their careers at a time when you worked hard, made your way up the corporate ladder, and often stayed at one employer your entire career. They tended to coach their Gen-X kids to "keep your nose clean, do good work, do the right thing by your employer, and you'll get rewarded." (This may actually help to explain some of the patterns we now see within the Gen-X segment.)

Now Boomers are retiring in droves—or at least planning to retire. And within this demographic there are far-ranging differences in wealth and readiness to retire. There's virtually a class of haves and have nots within this one cohort. Roughly half of them started saving early (far outclassing later generations in wealth accumulation) and will soon be responsible for the largest intergenerational wealth transfer in history. (Read on to see if the Millennials who stand to inherit that wealth will be poised to manage it wisely.) Yet half of them lack the money needed to retire with dignity and confidence, a problem only made worse as life expectancy has increased.

For the Boomers who aren't ready to retire and need to keep working, there is a real problem. It was already bad, as employers have begun nudging them out in favor of younger, less costly workers. But unexpected events like COVID have caused many of them to be unceremoniously booted out of the labor market. *Forbes* reported that in the first nine months of the pandemic, the number of Boomer-aged retirees increased by 1.1 million.[1] They need to keep working but there are fewer and fewer job opportunities for them.

Now, while there is a massive wealth transfer happening within generations as they retire, millions of them are struggling. We have an entire generation of Americans who are ill-equipped to retire. In particular, many of them may not be ready to retire even though it's "time." Many are understandably scared to run out of money. Their costs may be going through the roof while their earning power (and according to some, their productivity) is waning. Some employers may view them as "just hanging on" and may be eager to push any remaining Boomers out the door. But it's important to bear in mind that they started their careers in the era of pension plans and now they have self-directed 401(k) plans. That switch couldn't have been the easiest to make, but many of them adapted readily and set themselves up for comfortable retirements. But others are choosing to keep working or are lucky enough to have held on to their jobs and are lingering in the workforce, affecting the advancement and earning power of Gen Xers. They also have some very interesting views on employers, which are worth considering as you think about your employer brand promise, corporate social responsibility, and the role of financial wellness in society at large.

Baby Boomers have overwhelmingly lacked a plan when it comes to retirement. They have had extraordinary lives that have witnessed perhaps the greatest transformation of any global power and economy in history. So it's no wonder they have a retirement plan largely based on hope, Sunday services, and hard work.

Key stats on Boomers

- More than half are delaying retirement until seventy or later because of financial insecurity and rising health-care costs.[2]

- Sixty-six percent of retirees say their most recent employers did nothing to help with their transition to retirement, and another 16 percent were not sure how their employers helped.[3]

- Forty percent of Boomers and 51 percent of Gen Xers use mobile apps or online banking services as their primary banking channel.[4]

- They are retiring at a rate of 10,000 per day (before COVID).[5]

- Roughly half could retire in poverty or near poverty.[6]

- The average healthy sixty-five-year-old couple retiring in 2019–2020 is projected to spend more than $380,000 on health-care costs throughout retirement (not including long-term care).[7]

Myths and truths about Boomers

MYTH	TRUTH
Just coasting and unproductive	• Want to be engaged and eager to share tribal wisdom • Productive because they've mastered time management and know how to do more with less time • Often produce higher-quality work at a lower total cost
"Have it together" and are ready to ride off into the sunset	Anxious about retirement and still carry significant amounts of personal debt
Resistant to change	Just as adaptable as other workers if you help them understand the reason for change[8]

What Boomers need in order to improve their financial wellness

- Retirement income planning support and lifetime income solutions to help them convert 401(k) and pension savings into usable income they won't outlive

- Help in understanding Social Security and Medicare/Medicaid and how those factor into a retirement income plan that can last twenty to thirty years

- Contract or consulting work opportunities that leverage their deep experience

- Support groups or speakers with focused content such as retirement income or health care in retirement

- Legal assistance to help with matters such as estate planning

- Access to long-term care insurance and other solutions that can cushion the cost of health care in retirement

GEN X: forgotten, sandwiched, and struggling but highly resilient

Born: 1965–1980

Current age: 40–55

Where they need help: jugging financial demands as the "sandwich" generation and finding a reason to remain loyal to employers.

The context for Generation X provides a stark contrast with that of the Baby Boomers. Gen X lived through the 1980s, a more recent version of the 1920s, as well as economic turmoil, the fall of the Berlin Wall, the end of the Cold War, and a reinvigorated America, all while many saw their parents lose well-established, long-held jobs. They are the first generation forced to do DIY retirement planning as companies moved from defined benefit/pension plans to defined contribution plans that shifted the onus of retirement planning to employees.

The size of Gen X was constrained, as many were sons or daughters of hard-working immigrants. The parents of this generation worked hard, tried to be upwardly mobile, and valued a good education. My parents, immigrants from Wales, were loving, supportive, and tough. They truly wanted a better life than the coal mining mountains of Wales for their kids. And they love this country. I think that DNA and those values were ingrained in us Gen Xers. They repeatedly told their kids, "No one is going to do it for you." Gen Xers were not the generation that got a trophy for showing up. Not everyone is getting a trophy. They were taught that pain, loss, and suffering is how you learn and grow. My parents were perhaps the last generation that still remembers WWII, socialism, and the tough streets that helped build this country into an economic industrial power. A portion of this generation of Americans found themselves in poverty, which caused decreased birth rates, increased divorce rates, and increased abortions (following the legalization of abortion in the Supreme Court case Roe v. Wade).

Because of their somewhat challenging upbringing, many Gen Xers are resilient, excellent negotiators, strong leaders, and a little bit pessimistic.

They will take in feedback and enjoy building teams, but ultimately they are confident with making decisions that won't please everyone, and moving forward. They also earned a reputation as "apathetic, cynical, and anti-establishment."[9] This generation tries to balance work and life, allotting time to provide their children with the stable upbringing and financial security they never had. They strive to have fairly "portable" careers, where they see changing jobs as advantageous, educational, and necessary.

Gen Xers may be an increasingly frustrated group when it comes to how they're treated by employers. They're loyal and seasoned, but the fact that many of their elders are choosing to put off retirement (while Millennials are being promoted) may be preventing them from advancing. A 2019 study by the *Harvard Business Review* conducted a study with findings they called "unexpected": their hypothesis was that Gen Xers should be advancing rapidly and reaching the peaks of their careers. Instead, the study reveals that they're stalled out, often passed over in favor of Millennials (who sucked up virtually all of our attention in recent years) and also left without a seat at the leadership table as Boomers stay at work longer than ever.

While Millennials carry the greatest mass, employers should keep in mind that Gen X is still highly engaged and hard working. But they have fallen behind in some markers of financial maturity.[10] They are the new sandwich generation, juggling paying for their kids' college, caring for parents, and saving for retirement. They are natural capitalists, having started some of the world's most powerful tech companies, and they're natural skeptics who question authority and doubt they'll actually be able to rely on Social Security.

They were latchkey kids who survived without cell phones, roamed neighborhoods freely until dusk, and survived life before the Weather Channel and weather apps. They weathered tornado drills (and actual tornados) where school wasn't cancelled; rather, they were told to sit in the hall and put books over their heads or hide under their desks. But now they're under big pressure. They're starting to think about things like long-term care insurance for themselves while also caring for their aging parents.

After growing up seeing their parents earn a pension, it took a while for many to realize that saving for retirement was actually their own responsibility.[11] They are often known as the first generation to be less well off than their parents, with a median net worth that is lower than their predecessors.

They're tough but not invincible, and they could use some help in juggling their many financial burdens while they have a decent window of opportunity to prepare for retirement. They're basically in the thick of it financially, supporting themselves and their kids and parents to some degree while they at least still have solid earning power. Retirement simply hasn't come into clear focus for Gen X yet. The jury is still out on their long-term financial wellness. We will have a much better look at where they are from a savings standpoint in five years or so when they start turning sixty. At least they still have five to twenty years to get prepared for retirement.

While Generation X overall showed financial status indicators being below what they were for prior generations at their ages in 2016, the impact was *not* universal across Generation X. The families associated with disadvantaged groups were the driving force for the lower overall financial indicator results. In fact, the families with incomes in the upper two quartiles had nearly equal results to those of prior generations. However, the financial indicators for Generation X families with incomes in the lower two income quartiles were so much worse than for prior generations that they pulled down the overall results for Generation X. Furthermore, families with minority heads and heads without a bachelor's degree also did not fare as well as their counterparts after 2004.[12]

Key stats on Gen X

- They have an average of twenty years' experience and hold 51 percent of leadership roles worldwide.[13]

- Gen Xers are less likely to own a home than prior generations of the same age.[14]

- Sixty-six percent reported receiving only one promotion or no promotion (compared to 58 percent of Boomers and 52 percent of Millennials).[15]

- Forty percent are contemplating leaving to advance their careers.[16]

- Fifty-five percent of Gen X is behind schedule in saving for retirement.[17]

- Four in ten say that supporting their parents or in-laws is a cause of stress.[18]

- Debt-to-asset ratios for Gen-X-led families has climbed while median net worth has declined.

- If offered financial education programs at work, 89 percent would participate in them.[19]

- One-fourth say the desire for financial stability motivates them to stay in a job.[20]

- The top three topics on which they would seek advice: retirement planning, investing, and long-term care insurance.[21]

Myths and truths about Gen Xers

MYTH	TRUTH
Reliably loyal to employers	<ul><li>Increasingly restless as they get passed over for promotions and pay increases</li><li>Increasingly open to a job move</li></ul>
Not digitally savvy	Just as savvy as Millennials and can help bridge the digital divide in an organization[22]
Independent, solo actors, lone-wolf types	Open to advice from trusted sources such as career coaches and financial planners

What employers can do to help Gen Xers improve financial wellness

- Make sure salaries and promotions reflect actual value to the organization
- Put in place more objective hiring standards to prevent unconscious age bias
- Offer access to financial planning
- Broaden your financial protection benefits
- Offer self-service tools (they know how to use them)
- Offer solutions that help them deal with short-term cash and emergency needs such as extraordinary medical expenses

Millennials: the force comes of age

Born: 1980–1996

Current age: 24–40

Where they need help: managing debt, catching up financially, and improving overall financial literacy.

Millennials have been shamed, satirized, scoffed at, and caricatured for years now. If you do even five minutes of online research, it's evident the media was obsessed with them around 2013–2016. Pressured by their parents to begin building resumés in preschool, many Millennials are known to be high achieving, confident, driven, assertive, demanding, and self-centered. We also love to make fun of their helicopter parents . . . while possibly being one of them.

But guess what? They're older now, and they are the largest component in the U.S. labor force, approaching 100 million strong.

They tend to be natural-born joiners and are true digital natives fluent in technology. They often see themselves more as citizens of the world, priding themselves on thinking more globally than their predecessors. Many argue this reliance on technology has allowed Millennials to be uber connected but short on attention spans, while destroying interpersonal skills and causing a sense of isolation along with soaring depression and anxiety rates.

Time Magazine named Millennials "The Me Me Me Generation" because they want to do it all. Unfortunately, this has read to their elders as narcissistic and materialistic, and overconfident in all the wrong ways. They have a deeply etched reputation for being fans of group think, foosball, company bars, and are often mocked for demanding that work be fun above all. Remember, financial overconfidence is the worst of all worlds and can cause serious hardship across the board. We are seeing this manifest in student loan debt, credit card debt, and mortgages—that they can neither afford nor pay back.

In the workplace, Millennials want meaningful careers that make them feel like they are truly making a difference. They also want to know their employers are good corporate citizens in both internal and external affairs. As Punam Keller, Dean and Professor of Strategy, the Tuck School of Business, Dartmouth College, asserts, "If a company connects with the spirit or social consciousness of a Millennial, they will be loyal and true believers. This mindset is in part why Millennials want and expect their employers to offer financial wellness and other solutions. It would be otherworldly to imagine a Baby Boomer or Gen Xer asking the company CEO or CFO for personal financial advice. But coming from Millennials, it somehow doesn't surprise us."

Millennials and money

Like so many generations, Millennials show some fascinating complexity. They save and splurge on experiences and travel, and also have a reputation for splurging on boutique foods, pricey coffees, pricey experiences, and craft everything, from clothing to beer. After all, they brought us YOLO, FOMO, and emojis, shorthand culture where smiley faces and text shorthand found its way into business communications as an acceptable standard. Yet they also show an interesting level of caution and pragmatism about money under that luxe veneer. For example, a *Wall Street Journal* article pointed out that they might be quick to adopt apps, but then struggle to use them or abandon them because they don't understand them or know how to optimize them.

Even more interesting from that same *Wall Street Journal* article: "While Millennials are more comfortable than other generations using online tools for financial planning and to manage investments and other accounts, many also say they grapple with financial literacy." The article goes on to quote one user who tried a hot investing app but quickly closed the account "as she didn't have enough funds and wasn't well informed about which were the best ETFs or stocks to hold."

As Eric Milano at T. Rowe Price points out, "Research suggests that, in general, Millennials are worse off financially—on a like-for-like age comparison—than any generation since the so-called 'Greatest Generation' that suffered through the Great Depression."

In large part, that's the result of the Great Recession, and it's prompted a substantial change in mindset among that younger generation. But while Millennials may not be as wealthy on an inflation-adjusted basis as their grandparents were at the same age, there's a looming intergenerational wealth transfer that means they could come into money later.[23] There's a huge question about whether they'll be able to use that potential inheritance wisely. The financial wellness tools they access through employers will have a major effect on their future financial wellness and their ability to use any inherited assets to improve their financial standing.

Say what you will about Millennials—their size, scale, and diversity of thought are driving legislation, public policy, and workplace wellness solutions. Millennials not only want but expect their employers to provide financial wellness solutions for them. They look to the employer to help them with their health care, financial planning, retirement income planning, and student loan debt. They will be deeply loyal to employers who meet those needs. For the first time, we have a generation that is expecting the employer to provide benefits on demand, and in a way that makes sense and to help them with the budgeting and saving of their hard-earned money.

Millennials were born loving and expecting customization in virtually every part of their lives. They want to see this show up in financial tools provided to them by their employers and financial institutions.[24] And one of the most important things to bear in mind is that their careers got off to a slow start but now they feel like they need to make up for lost time and earn more, especially given how much student loan debt they carry.[25]

They're a surprisingly complex lot, and employees need to look past the stereotypes in order to truly understand them and meet their evolving needs. And the business case is undeniable: their refusal to settle for less drives up turnover costs for employers and bleeds $30.5 billion from the U.S. economy every year.[26]

Key stats on Millennials

- Twenty-two percent of Millennials say they have used mobile and online money managers like Betterment or Wealthfront, compared with just 4 percent of Baby Boomers and less than 3 percent of Gen Xers.

- Forty-six percent of Millennials say they prefer to learn about finance on a website, and only 25 percent would go to an in-person expert.

- Forty-four percent of Millennials turned down jobs that didn't offer the benefits they wanted.[27]

- Forty-five percent of Millennials have student loan debt.[28]

- Seventy-nine percent of Millennial employees are loyal to companies that care about their effect on society.[29]

- Millennials earn 20 percent less income than their parents.[30]

- Forty-six percent of Millennials surveyed say they aren't saving enough money and 39 percent say they expect to be forced to work beyond retirement age.[31]

- Sixteen percent of Millennials aged between twenty-three and thirty-seven have already saved $100,000 in their accounts for retirement.[32]

- More than half of Millennials rate employee benefits as one of the most important factors in their decision to stay with their current employers.[33]

- Millennials (defined here as ages twenty-four to forty) have racked up an average of $27,900 in personal debt.[34]

- About 51 percent of Millennials say their overall financial situation is lagging compared to where it should be—and 60 percent feel behind specifically when it comes to retirement savings.

- Only 44 percent have an emergency savings fund that can cover at least three months of living expenses.

- Forty-nine percent have a 401(k) and roughly one in four Millennials have a Roth IRA.[35]

- While many say they grapple with financial literacy, three out of four Millennials say they're currently saving in some capacity, and they started saving much earlier (age twenty-four) than their Baby Boomer parents (age thirty-three).[36]

Myths and truths about Millennials

MYTH	TRUTH
Disloyal job hoppers	• As loyal as other generations, but more demanding • Will readily change employers if expectations are misaligned or not met

Unfocused and lazy	• Good at multitasking
	• Inquisitive
	• Lifelong learners
	• Want to work smarter, not harder, and they deplore inefficiency and bureaucracy[37]
Only live for today	• Also focused on the future and value benefits like retirement plans
	• Risk averse and pragmatic about money and saving
Starry-eyed and blindly optimistic	• Skeptical
	• Untrusting of large financial institutions and being "sold" by sales reps
	• Prefer transparency and straight talk

How employers can help Millennials improve financial wellness

- Student loan debt relief
- Apps and self-service digital tools supported with robust educational elements
- General financial literacy and planning support
- Offer multimedia, interactive tools to satisfy their digital-first natures and engage them
- Use refreshingly honest messaging in your education efforts
- Demonstrate how financial wellness benefits have a positive impact on society

What about Gen Z (a.k.a. "Zoomers")?

The truth is, it's a bit too early to tell about Gen Z because they haven't fully entered the workforce yet. Definitions vary, but organizations such as Pew Research define them as anyone born after 1997. But foremost, they are pure digital natives, and they'll put tremendous pressure on employers to deliver a highly differentiated digital experience in every aspect of work. They seem to be focused and willing to work their tails off for what they want. My kids happen to be in this group, and I think a lot of people in my age range can agree they give off a very different vibe than Millennials. They may be a smaller segment than Millennials, but as you think about your longer-range workforce and benefits planning, don't expect them to be any less influential or driven unless and until they prove themselves otherwise.

Global consultancy McKinsey offers an interesting summary of Zoomers, defining them as those born from 1995–2010 and describing them as a "hypercognitive generation very comfortable with collecting and cross-referencing many sources of information and with integrating virtual and offline experiences." McKinsey goes on to describe them as a generation that values dialogue, rejects stereotypes, and is pragmatic.

Let's put it this way: from the impression I'm gathering so far, I'd be more afraid to go toe-to-toe in a debate with a Zoomer than a Millennial. I have friends with kids of all ages, and I think the toddlers and the Zoomers are the ones who could outwit most of us adults most effectively right now. It will be exciting to see how this cohort evolves and influences the world, including the world of work.

Implications for employers

The question for employers is what to do with the demographic information available to you, and why it matters. In working with employers across the country, part of my job is to help employers put data, trends, and stereotypes into perspective, then figure out how to translate them into business and operations strategies. Regardless of the size of your staff, your sophistication level, or your industry, devoting some time to demographics at large and within your employee base can have enormous benefit. It will help your human capital management, total rewards programs, career pathing and mentorship, departmental succession planning, and morale. In addition, there are a number of benefits where having this understanding will help drive better outcomes for employees. Among them:

- **Demographics can help you form solid hypotheses about a group.** This gives you a starting point, somewhere to aim your gaze as you think about your benefits strategy. It reduces guesswork and helps you make some starting assumptions about a given segment of your employee population.

- **Demographics can be used to create greater empathy within your management teams and gives you more empathy for the various cohorts you employ today and in the future.** There is a bit of duality at play here. On one hand, demographics can help you see commonalities across groups and understand the many ways people are more alike than different. At the same time, demographics can help you see some of the subtle distinctions within groups that you might have otherwise been callous to or unaware of altogether. For example, we know there are glaring inequalities in financial wellness: women and minorities tend to carry a much higher student loan debt burden, people of color tend to experience greater financial stress, women were hit especially hard with job losses and being forced out of the workforce during the COVID-19 pandemic… just to name a few examples.

- **Demographics can help you tailor your financial wellness benefits for greatest impact, equity, inclusivity, and efficiency.** By making strategic use of demographics, you can first find the common denominators: which benefits will have the broadest impact? From there, you can use demographics to avoid the "kitchen sink" phenomenon of offering every cool voluntary benefit under the sun and zero in on the added benefits that are most likely to improve outcomes for your employees, and which help to address disparities in financial wellness across gender, ethnicity, and other groups within your employee base. This more strategic approach can also help ensure you're offering benefits that are actually worth the cost and effort it takes your teams to administer. In this way, the financial wellness benefits you choose to offer can have a substantive, measurable impact on your diversity, inclusion, and equality initiatives. Framing benefits through this lens with your employees can also help them better understand why these benefits are important to understand and embrace. Above all, recognize that we're facing an intergenerational financial struggle. It's evident that every generation currently in the workforce is grappling with significant financial challenges. These challenges are not going away and, increasingly, they are only crossing over generations. The tools may be different to combat these issues across an employee segment, but the broader remedy is the same. We need to address underlying issues in order to create better outcomes. The more employers can do to help each generation improve their financial wellness, the more the employer is helping themselves, the individuals, and society as a whole. Anything that can be done to reduce slack in the system, reduce financial stress, and provide targeted solutions will help employees, create a more productive workforce, help businesses improve margins, and continue to push out inefficiencies.

- **Use demographics to steer your benefits strategy, but be careful about falling into the traps of bucketing and mass stereotyping.** In an era where empathy matters more than ever, it's critical to remember there are humans behind all the numbers and stereotypes. As American workers increasingly look to employers as trusted life and wellness coaches, this is more important than ever. Demographics merely provide solid generalizations and serve as a sort of helpful shortcut. It's also important to talk to your people. Meet with them, engage them. Ask them what they are struggling with the most and what they need and expect from you as their employer. I'm not suggesting that employees should dictate strategy, but their perceptions about their own needs and wants is one important input among many that you should consider. While it's important to bear in mind that statistics and behavioral economics tell us people may not always understand money or what they need, surveys may be able to put a human face on financial wellness and help confirm or deny hypotheses you and your advisors may have based on the solid science of demographics.

In a 2015 article, "Myths about Millennials," *The Economist* wisely warned that businesses should "beware of dubious generalizations . . . . Companies need to recognize that individual differences are always bigger than generational differences."

- Smaller companies, which may be busy doing basic blocking and tackling and answering routine questions (like, "How do I enroll in my 401(k)?") may also not have the staff or bandwidth to leverage all this. The most important point is to be cognizant of demographics. And ask your vendor partners and consultants how they're leveraging demographics on your behalf. They can help you choose benefits that will have the broadest applicability, or if they are highly targeted or customized, ensure you're targeting with the greatest impact for employees and ROI for your business.

- Just as with other strategic planning and data, using demographics can help you be more on target with what you're offering today and what will be most relevant to your employee base in the near and short term.

- Hyper-targeted interventions or offerings by generation may not be overly effective, so don't over-index on them.[38] With just a little planning and leveraging data, you can better tailor your benefits offering. You might even be able to save time or money by removing benefits that are not all that valued by employees. They can also be used to help the entire C-suite understand the right mix of benefits. In some cases, you may be so busy running around doing your job you may not even know the average age of your employee base.

- You may not be sure what data you have and how to leverage it. Your consultants and vendor partners can help you determine your employee demographics and how they can or should affect your benefits strategy.

- Step back and ask yourself what are some small ways you can be applying demographic data in order to better meet the needs of your current and future employees.

- You're going to take the data you have, look at your employee base, and make decisions that work best for your business.

- Talk to your employees. See what they need now and what they think they are going to need two, three, or five years from now.

- Use demographics to hone your strategy. For example, you can offer dozens of low-volume-use voluntary benefits that you're having to invest resources in educating employees to understand and use, or you can sharpen up your offering by triangulating your employee's greatest needs, their potential impact, and the efficiency of administration.

At the end of the day, we are talking about our work family. We want to be able to support them and understand them. We should and can do a better job of that, frankly. We see and work with them every day. Let's use what we have at our disposal to better understand who our colleagues are, working side-by-side with us. Sure, we have lunch with them, have holiday parties, celebrate birthdays, but if we aren't working to create better outcomes, then the rest of our efforts ring hollow and become purely for commercial gain. I think it's fair to say we want more than that for ourselves, our colleagues, and our businesses.

Questions to consider

- Do we have a detailed understanding of the demographics of our employee base?

- What percentage of our employees will or should ideally be retiring in the next five years?

- Do we have a plan in place to help Boomers generate and manage retirement income?

- What is our strategy for employees nearing retirement (e.g., buyout strategy or other)?

- Do we have a strategy and specific, relevant solution for each of the segments of our employee population? Solutions for each cohort—a strategy and a plan for each segment of our population?

- Do we have a solid handle on our current census and demographics?

- How have our employee demographics changed and have we planned specifically for how they might change in the future?

- How are we interacting with each demographic segment when it comes to wellness? Do we understand important differences not only across age groups, but across racial and ethnic segments of our employee base?

- How are we educating our employees on budgeting, planning, debt management, emergency savings, digital advice, financial wellness apps, and retirement income planning?

| 7 |

The Changing Relationship Between Employer and Employee: From Business Contract to Mutual Social Contract

"People try to convince you that you should keep your empathy out of your career. Don't accept this false premise."

—Tim Cook, CEO, Apple

Over the past two centuries, the only constant in the employer-employee relationship has been change. And that change has been coming at a faster and faster pace. Just in the past decade after the Great Recession, we've seen periods of booming economic growth, stock market accelerations, low unemployment, the full integration of Millennials into the workforce, and the explosion of technology and digital mobile technologies. That's led to periods of incredibly stiff competition in the war to attract and retain talent. While employees still provide labor, skills, and expertise in return for money, the view that employees are a mere commodity has all but gone the way of the dinosaur. The employer-employee relationship has entered a new era of empathy and interdependence. Changing mindsets in the C-suite and changing needs and expectations from employees-as-consumers have come together in a top-down, bottom-up push to transform the workplace into the front line for of all employee wellness. Especially financial wellness.

Nowhere has this been more evident than in the HR benefits function. Benefits-related technology has exploded; employees have come to expect an ever-expanding array of benefits, and the domain of responsibility and complexity for HR decision-makers only continues to increase. More importantly, the currency exchange in the employer-employee relationship has changed drastically. Workplace wellness and its heightened importance for the employee has catapulted the social contract between employer/employee to levels never seen before and has forever changed the interdependence between these seemingly varied company cohorts. The construct has come from boards, executives, and human resource committees throughout the country. But make no mistake, the directive is coming from both directions—top down and bottom up. The interconnectivity is the lifeline that will continue to elevate the best employees in a new world, with new technology, know-how, empathy, resilience, and demographics.

Why here and why now? How did we get to this point, where technology-enabled financial wellness solutions would be distributed through the employer? That clearly wasn't the conventional wisdom until very, very recently. First, personal financial situations are, well, personal. Second, technology for the past twenty-five years has either been consumer-facing or enterprise-wide serving. Think Facebook, Google, SAP, Microsoft, Salesforce. Employers were not the logical vessels through which individual-facing technology, applications, or consulting were offered. After all, these were employees—they worked. Why would anyone think that they had any additional time to better expand their financial literacy, budgeting, planning, debt service, or additional savings strategies? The relationship had to change to make this a reality. It wasn't logical or a given that this was going to happen at all. Not at all.

How did we get here?

Two parts of this equation needed to evolve. And just like George Clooney in *The Perfect Storm*, many, many things had to come into focus, ideas had to evolve, technology had to be easy to grasp, employees had to actually want these services and, lastly, the corporate culture had to embrace these changes, make social impact a priority, and realize that a financially healthier employee makes for a much more resilient and loyal workforce. From here, it's all about execution and communication.

It's fascinating, really. There's no way any of this could have come together two, five, or ten years ago. We reached a perfect moment in time where employers were ready, technology was ready to enable delivery, and employees were in need and becoming more demanding. As we mentioned in the introduction to this section on megatrends, these tectonic forces converged to make the employer, by far, the most perfect distribution channel for financial wellness solutions. It's also become absolutely obvious that the employer is, by far, the most logical distribution outlet for individual financial wellness solutions delivered rapidly and at scale. It's much like the idea of the steam engine. Inventors dabbled with the idea of harnessing steam power for hundreds of years. But greater, faster developments began to occur in the seventeenth century, and suddenly by the eighteenth century, the need and the capability came about and steam became central to the Industrial Revolution.[1] Financial wellness' time has come. The time has come for the employer to become the primary caregiver of wellness-related solutions to a vast majority of Americans.

To some degree, employers still view employees as human capital and a component in the supply chain. Employees are resources, after all. But the employer-employee relationship has become more "human" than at virtually any other time in modern history. And whereas employers have generally held much of the power in the relationship (especially during periods of rising unemployment), the balance of power has become much more equalized. The tables have turned and, in many cases, employees hold much of the power. They are sitting with a royal flush.

Newer generations expect more and more from employers in terms of benefits, and employers are being forced to offer more benefits in order to remain competitive. I can't count how many meetings I've been in with HR veterans who continue to express shock over how much their roles have changed over the years. The HR benefits function doesn't look anything like it did even ten years ago.

The rise of employee assistance programs also has reflected the need for a warmer employer embrace and resources that didn't exist before the Millennials entered the workforce two decades ago.

We've moved well out of an era of a financial contract, where employees were seen purely as resources to benefit the company. We're now squarely in an era where the relationship between the two is much more of a mutual social contract, even empathetic and paternal—driven as much by the employee's changing wants and needs as by the employer's business needs. One of the most obvious manifestations of this change is the rapid growth of workplace financial wellness programs.

This has been a gradual and logical shift as financial literacy has decreased, the number of fintech solutions has exploded, life expenses such as medical care have skyrocketed, the burden of retirement planning has shifted to the employee, and as external events like the COVID pandemic reveal just how economically fragile many American workers and their employers really are.

Especially during times of uncertainty, employers and the financial wellness solutions they provide employees can serve as ballast to tens of millions of working Americans—helping them stay upright and navigate the financial storms and complexities of life. In turn, employees who see their employers as caring and concerned about their financial welfare are often more loyal and more productive. They'll in turn be more likely to stand by the employer during challenging times. Both are made more resilient as a result. This has been particularly evident during the COVID pandemic, as employees at companies such as Delta Air Lines and countless others that have a strong employer brand have willingly accepted compromises such as temporary pay cuts and furloughs in order to help keep their employers solvent.

At no time in history have the employer and employee needed each other more. And at no time in history have Americans expected more from their employer as a source of complete wellness solutions. The relationship between employer and employee has become much more about mutual loyalty, empathy, mutual regard for welfare, and connectivity.

There's simply a soul to the employer-employee relationship that hasn't been there in the past, at least not in the way it is now. It's also become absolutely obvious that the employer is by far the most logical distribution outlet for individual financial wellness solutions delivered rapidly and at scale.

Let's take a closer look at what's behind this evolution.

Key moments in the employer-employee relationship

Countless changes and milestone events have occurred that shaped the dynamic between employers and employees. Some of them are subtle, while others have led to fairly radical changes in the workplace benefits landscape.

Money and retirement		Health and medical
• 1848—first disability insurance launched in England	Late 1800s	
• Early 1900s—employer-sponsored retirement plans emerge	Early 1900s	
• Revenue Acts pave way for pension and profit sharing plans • 1935 – Social Security Act	1920—1930s	

• 1950s—1960s—Pension plan regulations protect workers	1940s—1950s	• 1940s – Modern era of employer-sponsored health insurance begins • Programs to treat work-related alcoholism become precursors of EAPs
• 1974—ERISA enacted • 1978—401(k) tax code introduced	1960s—1970s	HDHPs born
• McDonald's launches first 401(k) auto enrollment	1980s—1990s	
	Early 2000s	HSAs and FSAs become integrated with HDHPs
• 2006—Pension Protection Act creates safe harbor provision	Mid 2000s	
• 2015—Richard Thaler wins Nobel Prize, thrusting behavioral economics into mainstream • 2016—financial wellness movement emerges • 2019—Student loan repayments become tax deductible	2010s—2021	2014—Affordable Care Act (ACA) introduced
• Expanded student loan debt relief • Workplace case savings plans	*Future state*	Coverage for caretakers

Sources:
1 https://en.wikipedia.org/wiki/Disability_insurance
2 https://www.soa.org/globalassets/assets/library/newsletters/health-watch-newsletter/2019/february/hsn-2019-iss88-busch.pdf

As a 2020 LinkedIn article points out, employers are seeing ever-dwindling, declining pensions (unless you are in the public, education, or government sectors), increased financial worries, and the colossal chasm in financial literacy. (In fact, pensions are all but dead. Not declining, but largely nonexistent. Take out public, government, and union plans, and they are few and far between.) They also see the massive financial stress employees are under and what that costs to business in lost productivity, increased health-care costs, and more. It says, "Companies are investing in new ways" to reduce employee financial stress. Providers like Fidelity Investments have focused deliberately for the past five years on expanding their financial wellness programs offered to employees. It's important to point out that, again, if you ask twelve people what financial wellness is, you get twelve different answers and that's true regardless of who you are talking to— Fidelity or Kolcraft, a leading manufacturer of children's strollers and crib mattresses based in Chicago. In fact, more than twice as many companies are offering these plans today. That's 53 percent today compared to only 24 percent five years ago.[2]

Empathetic leadership: rising awareness for the plight of others

Regardless of what may seem like momentary or surface divisions, it's fair to say that, on the whole, we've become much more empathetic as a society. Perhaps it's because of the widespread availability of technology and the rise of multimedia storytelling and social media that have all enabled us to see the world through the eyes of others much more readily. And certainly events like large-scale regional natural disasters and COVID have also shown us that we are much more alike than different. We have also become more empathetic because the largest portion of the workforce is struggling financially and is longing for that support, help, and guidance. If we don't have willing, receptive parties on both sides, empathetic businesses or conscious capitalism would fall on deaf ears and not gain traction.

Consider companies like Boeing, UPS, Blackrock, and Voya. Each have realized the business and human reasons to begin offering employees the option to divert a portion of their pay to short-term emergency fund savings plans. "This kind of innovation would not have happened under the old paradigm, before we began thinking differently about financial wellness and had more advanced capabilities for deploying targeted solutions right to the source of a problem," says Michael D'Ambrose, Executive Vice President and CHRO at Boeing. Likewise, Blackrock and Voya teamed up to provide a short-term emergency savings initiative for one of their clients, United Parcel Service (UPS), to address the same underlying issue of a lack of employee short-term savings.

There is a rising consciousness of the plight of others—not only among everyday individuals, but among employers. One of the most interesting and influential announcements around the role of the employer in our society was released in 2019 by the Business Roundtable Association. Jamie Dimon, Chair of this association and Chairman and CEO of JP Morgan, and 180 of his peers on the Roundtable, announced that the role and responsibilities of a CEO and a board of directors had expanded. Their statement asserted that the responsibility of corporate employers is not to provide a mere contract with their employees, or focus on margins, profits, or enhancing shareholder value. It's more than that. It now includes employee well-being, mental health support, corporate citizenship, sustainability, and access support and resources needed to improve financial literacy. In other words, for the first time since model corporate governance, corporate finance, and securities laws were enacted in the 1940s, the masters of the corporate universe acknowledged that companies should be willing to sacrifice margin, profitability, and returns in order to improve individual outcomes. The statement reads, in part:

America's businesses have been a critical engine to its success.

Yet we know that many Americans are struggling. Too often, hard work is not rewarded, and not enough is being done for workers to adjust to the rapid pace of change in the economy.

If companies fail to recognize that the success of our system is dependent on inclusive long-term growth, many will raise legitimate questions about the role of large employers in our society.[3]

But that's not to say the relationship between employer and employee has turned to a chummy friendship. As the Corporate Leadership Board pointed out in 2019, "Most firms have become consumers of labor versus nurturers of talent, as part of a growing 'supply chain' mentality toward labor."[4] Granted, this was before COVID forced us to all jump in the same lifeboat. But the employers who will surface as winners in the war for talent and the best corporate citizens will be the ones who don't give in to this dehumanizing view, and who continue to balance business pressures with a very human approach to their employees and to the benefits they offer.

Fred Barstein, Founder and Executive Director of The Retirement Advisor University (TRAU), spends a great deal of time writing and talking to plan consultants about the evolving relationship between employees and employers. "Employers are recognizing the connection between employee financial wellness, employee morale, employee engagement, and the resiliency and total health of the employee and the business organisms," he explains. Barstein also firmly believes that employers really can do well by doing good. "Just as with selling a product or service, if you are doing it just to make money, then it's not sustainable," he says. "If you're viewing an employee as merely an asset vehicle to commercial gain, you have it all wrong, and that is going to catch up with you."

The role of employer brand, reputation, and employee experience design

Another interesting factor contributing to the focus on employees and benefits as part of their total experience with your company may be the rise of customer experience design as a discipline. In the mid-2000s or so, when CX and the voice of customer programs and design thinking became all the rage, the employee experience was naturally thrust under a spotlight. After all, employees are your first and most important customer. And their experience with and sentiments toward you as an employer will be reflected directly in their ability to empathize with and serve your company's external customers. It reminded employers that employees are really your first and most important customers. Give employees a good experience and they will, in turn, give your customers a good experience.

This is one reason you have to care about employees, even if deep down you or members of your team may think it's not a big deal. In an era when empathy, transparency, and immediacy are infiltrating every part of our lives, you have to place a priority on employees. I speak to employers all the time, and on rare occasion I see one who is perfectly happy to ignore even basic best practices and offer employees sub-par benefits. Within any given leadership or management team, some will say they want to do it. Others do not. Others don't care. You have to care . . . these are the problems people are bringing to work with them. Empathy matters.

I met with an employer recently who offers hardly any benefits and has no desire to offer more expanded financial wellness benefits. Candidly, the ownership just doesn't care. And what do they see as a result of that harsh, apathetic view of the employees who keep the company running? They see high turnover, low job satisfaction, unhealthy employees who are distracted, physically ill from financial stress, and horrid reviews on Glassdoor and LinkedIn. For employers like this, old-school thinking will create old-school results, and they may end up running the business into the ground. We're in a new era of mutual accountability. It doesn't mean employees get to call all the shots, but it does mean their demographic context and the very real needs and struggles they bring to work each day simply can't be ignored.

BEHAVIOR NUDGES

Tunneling

If there's an emergency, we can only think about the emergency. This is one reason employers should do everything possible to help employees be prepared for financial emergencies, which can cause enormous personal and professional distractions and disruptions.

Why empathy matters to Millennials

Empathy-based leadership has also played a major role in management's ability to align itself with its employees. This is particularly important for the Millennial cohort. If management can demonstrate a real sense of purpose in its business and also demonstrate sincere empathy—a kind of window into its soul—then employees will not only be attracted to a particular company, but have been shown to stay longer and remain loyal to the employer.

Millennials naturally gravitate and affix to this newer, more empathetic leadership style, as their whole lives have been largely guided, coddled, rewarded, and highly programmed. They want to know they are heard, seen, and understood. That is not meant to belittle Millennials. It is just that Jamie Dimon's empathy-based listening and leadership with a consciousness would have fallen on deaf ears with the cynical and pragmatic Gen X. And the Boomer executives who were their managers early in their careers would have told them to pull themselves up by their bootstraps and just do their jobs.

For example, would I have walked into my managing director's office when I was an up-and-coming investment banker and asked his thoughts on where I should invest my money or how best to consolidate my student loans? Not unless I wanted him to throw a paperweight or lucite in my direction and tell me to re-run the leveraged buyout model looking at a whole host of new scenarios, cap tables, interest rates, and multiples. Would I have argued on the Thanksgiving Day when he demanded we all be at work in the bullpen on the eve of a big merger? No way. But times are different. People are different. And today's leadership norms, coupled with the needs and personality traits of the Millennials, dovetail in time and space to align perfectly. I can still remember the comment, "DB, there will be other Thanksgivings. There is only one XYZ merger." I bought into it hook, line, and sinker. I had no choice.

The employer-employee relationship is, in a sense, coming full circle. We are implementing change at a breakneck pace: uprooting standards, traditions, and workplace orthodoxy that was once viewed as sacred or impossible to change. In many ways, it's enormously progressive and forward-thinking as the employer and the employee lean side-by-side into this new future. And yet, it's fascinating that in many ways it harkens back to the early twentieth century, when the employer was a magnet, center of life, and focal point for a working community both socially and economically.

Size and scale: why employers of all sizes have to care

I understand why some employers may think they can't afford to forge a different relationship with employees by offering more, and more meaningful, financial wellness benefits. But rest assured, there are cost-effective options out there that you *can* feasibly implement regardless of your size or industry. In fact, the smaller you are, the less you can afford to ignore it, because the cost of absorbing turnover and distractions takes a much greater toll on a smaller employer. Mingee Kim, a Senior Vice President at HUB International and leading benefits expert, says, "Whether you are a small employer with under one-hundred employees or a large national or multinational business, we're seeing some very universal shifts in employer concern for employee welfare, and the need for in-depth communication about benefits that goes much deeper than a few lunchtime meetings." She believes the shift toward remote working is going to create a drastic shift in what's needed for authentic employee engagement and productivity. "Employers who figure that out and look beyond the commercial aspect of the employer-employee relationship, and who embrace the new currency, are going to be winners over time. While we all had a blast at work from 2010–2019 with cereal bars, indoor volleyball courts, nap pods, and foosball tables, that's not what employees want anymore," she explains.

Winning at hiring and retention in the new workplace paradigm

The world of work is changing in countless ways. For instance, in the post-COVID era, it's highly likely that remote work will be much more commonplace. Some aspects of life and work may normalize, but many of the changes seen in the workplace can never be walked back.

As *HR Executive* pointed out in an article from Chris Pyne of Unum, increased remote working "will increase the war for talent." He explains, "When people can work anywhere, their choice of employers is virtually unlimited. To compete, employers will need to revisit their benefits offerings, even if the economy is slow to recover."

Charlie Nelson, a veteran and thought leader in retirement plan administration and now CEO of Retirement and Employee Benefits for Voya Financial, Inc. has a stunningly clear way of putting the value of employees in perspective. He says, "Financial capital used to be costly, something that you treasured and were very careful about how you deployed. But today, financial capital is relatively cheap. And I don't care how much tech or AI or robotics you deploy, what's more priceless—and a make-or-break in your business growth—is your human capital and your labor pool." Thus, he says, "It's in the best interests of your business to step right into the arena of financial wellness so you stand a fighting chance of attracting and retaining the talent you're going to need to succeed."

The relationship between employer and employee has matured, in a sense. Employers who embrace and understand this new dynamic will be the ones who emerge prepared not only to attract and keep employees, but to help those employees improve their financial outcomes with meaningful financial wellness benefits.

As it always has, the relationship between employer and employee will continue to evolve. But doing nothing and sticking your head in the sand is not an option. The more you do to keep a pulse on things, the better off your business will be. We don't know what the future holds. But we do know the employer has the power and, frankly, the privilege to serve as a powerful stabilizing force for employees in their journey to financial wellness. Who knows, perhaps the next-gen financial wellness benefit will be reduced-cost access to tax planning software or advice as employees take on the overhead cost of running home offices and businesses reduce their physical footprint. We can't say for sure, but the point is to have your eyes open to how the relationship is evolving. And push your advisors and vendor partners to keep you abreast of changing dynamics. You can rest assured that if you're not paying attention to it, your competitor will be.

While some of this may seem daunting, I find it inspiring and exciting above all else. Employers have the ability to be impactful, to truly make a difference in the lives of their employees and ultimately change their life trajectories and outcomes. And, for the first time, they have a receptive, expectant, and deeply appreciative employee base. That's a powerful position to be in. It's a privilege, and one we should embrace.

Questions to consider

- How has our company's role in the lives of our employees changed or expanded?

- Are we as prepared as we need to be to understand what financial wellness benefits our employee are going to want and expect from us, and are we prepared to respond quickly?

- What training are we offering to our benefits teams to help them anticipate the financial wellness needs of our employees? Are we offering our benefits team the data to help them anticipate trends and needs?

- How has our relationships with our employees changed, and how do we see it changing in the future?

- Have we reflected on how it's changed over the years?

- Are we prepared for the 100 million Millennials who are only now integrating into the workforce?

THE UNDENIABLE FORCE OF BEHAVIORAL ECONOMICS: THE SCIENCE AND ART OF HUMANS AND THEIR MONEY

"Wouldn't economics make a lot more sense if it were based on how people actually behave, instead of how they should behave?"

—Dan Ariely, Professor of Psychology and Behavioral Economics, Duke University

Behavioral economics. What manager or HR director would have thought fifty years ago that those two words would come together and ultimately become one of the most important, most innovative, and most transformative disciplines of the modern era?

There has now been more than four decades of research around social science, neuroscience, economics, psychology, and organizational behavior that have all come together under the umbrella now commonly known as behavioral economics. This field looks at how humans make decisions, why they make those decisions, and the effects those decisions have on themselves, their families, and peers—and, most importantly, their money and their financial wellness. Sitting at the intersection of all that, with a bird's-eye view, are behavioral economists.

This area of study has influenced public policy, shaped the financial industry, and encouraged the offering of financial wellness solutions through the most logical channel of all: employers.

As Richard Thaler, Nobel prize-winning University of Chicago professor and widely recognized as the proverbial godfather of behavioral economics explains it, this entire field aims to "improve decisions about health, wealth, and happiness."

In this chapter, we can't possibly do a complete exploration of the vast and important work that has been and is being done in this fast-growing, critically important field. Nor can we do it full justice in summary form. But what we can do is share some highlights we think are most useful as you think about your employee benefits and how you can help employees improve their own financial wellness.

Understanding behavioral economics is critical to understanding how people make financial decisions that affect their personal and professional lives. The biggest driver of how individuals make decisions as it relates to money—how they save or spend it—as well as how they run toward or away from risk, can be traced to the fundamentals of behavioral economics. Behavioral economics, when combined with demographics and elements of social science, has had the single biggest impact on how we not only understand how our employees prioritize financial decisions and how they relate to money, but also how employers and public policy (in the form of tax policy, in particular) can provide the road map to help improve financial wellness for individuals.

Why employers should care about behavioral economics

Behavioral economics recognizes, above all, that consumers are irrational, overconfident, and supremely human when it comes to how they handle money. It also recognizes that humans can be predictably illogical about money. Yet the truth is, many workplace wellness programs still rely on rational thought rather than on the reality of human irrationality toward money.[1]

Those companies that take active steps to recognize and understand how their employees make financial decisions, by understanding the basics of behavioral economics—layered on top of basic demographic information—will be best positioned to make the highest and best use of both the insights they yield, and to attract and retain top talent now and in the years ahead.

This is not to say that you or members of your team need to become experts in behavioral economics.

But what you can do is benefit from the vast wisdom of the countless experts in this field in order to design more effective benefits programs and improve financial outcomes for your employees and, ultimately, your business. By taking a bit of time to learn or brush up on behavioral economics, you'll gain more information about yourself, and those around you, and have much more empathy and insight as you design and deploy employee benefits programs. You'll have new levels of insight into the fears and anxieties that employees are faced with on a daily basis. And you'll also gain a better understanding of some of the foibles and weaknesses we all have when it comes to money. (Yes, even financial experts like myself.)

Behavioral economics 101

Behavioral economics is an academic field of study that analyzes how human emotion, inherent biases, and our behavior affect how we make decisions across an entire array of things. It looks at how we run toward or away from risk. It looks at how our emotions, impulses, and fears affect how we make decisions. It looks at how we, as humans, can be absolutely brilliant and full of common sense in some ways but melt into a puddle of irrationality and poor judgment when any amount of money or reward is at stake.

It looks at why we buy high and sell low. Why we find ways to justify taking out loans to pay for things we can't actually afford. Why we spend today when we know we need to be saving for the future. Why we have a built-in bias for the car that's more expensive than the car that has a better safety record. The list could go on ad infinitum.

By investing just a bit of energy to make ourselves current on behavioral economics and understanding what the leading minds in behavioral economics are working on and thinking about, we come as close as we can to looking into a crystal ball and seeing what could be in the next two, five, ten, or twenty years. That's because it's been shown over and over that behavioral economists are, to some degree, our modern-day version of sages and soothsayers. Many of the current programs, technologies, and program designs that help individuals financially budget and plan, save money, invest that money, pay back student loans, prepare for financial emergencies and for retirement were born out of research done decades ago at the University of Chicago, Stanford, Dartmouth College, Duke University, UCLA, and other pillars of academia by some of the earliest behavioral economists when the field was moving from infancy to adolescence.

We still have much to learn in terms of understanding the principles of behavioral economics and how to apply them for real benefit to society and businesses. In fact, when I teach my Plan Sponsor University fiduciary governance class at the University of Chicago or Vanderbilt University, if I ask most classes a simple question as to why we have vesting schedules, automatic 401(k) enrollment, stretch match provisions, and other staples in the HR world, I'm often met with blank stares. One of the things I love most about teaching is sharing my excitement over behavioral economics and what it has brought to the world and continues to bring us. The fact is, so much of the structural plan design provisions and related legislation that have been proposed and brought to fruition—including the groundbreaking Pension Protection Act, SECURE Act, CARES Act, and more—have virtually all come from the cradle of academic research and this particular field of study. So let's start at the source and take a brief look into how behavioral economics has influenced the employer-employee relationship and benefits design to support better outcomes for people like you and me.

The history of behavioral economics

Humans have been interacting with money for millennia. And our behaviors toward that money have been reliably and consistently surprising, amusing, and often irrational. Our funny relationship with money is nothing new. But what is fairly new in the scheme of things is the field of behavioral economics. While psychology, social science, and economics have been studied for decades, it's only been in the last thirty to forty years that behavioral economics has transcended those silos, joined elements of each, and emerged as a profession in its own right.

Given just how important this field has become, it's stunning to realize that it wasn't until 2017 that the first Ph.D. program in behavioral economics was launched.[2] That's how new this field is in the world of economics. And in 2017, *Harvard Business Review* (*HBR*) was still referring to behavioral economics as "a relatively new field that combines insights from psychology, judgment and decision-making, and economics to generate a more accurate understanding of human behavior."[3]

As I discussed in Chapter 1, it was only in 2008 that Thaler, together with Cass Sunstein, wrote a book called *Nudge: Improving Decisions about Health, Wealth, and Happiness*, which proposed it's possible to "nudge" people's behavior by understanding and influencing how they make decisions. That book and the ideas in it had rapid, broad impact that influenced thinking in multiple fields, including employee benefits design. Nudges come in various shapes and sizes—environmental issues, socially responsible investing, or eating healthier. Nudges can also come from either the private sector or the government. The government can have a heavy hand, if it so chooses, to direct people to act and behave a certain way and, in more subtle ways, pass public policy (laws) that encourage and incentivize companies and individuals.

Field of geniuses: giants in the field of behavioral economics

There are countless experts, social scientists, and mere observers we could recognize in this field. But a few of them stand out as absolute pillars in the field, and if you spend any amount of time studying it, you'll run into them over and over again. Some of them have gained near-celebrity status, while others may toil away quietly their entire careers and never receive public recognition.

Whether they achieve fame or not, as a financial expert I truly believe the world owes them a debt of gratitude for what they can teach us about ourselves and each other as we all grapple to understand ourselves and those around us and why we behave or misbehave as we do when it comes to money.

They are right now thinking about the things you and I will thank them for ten years from now for teaching us today. They've given us an entire field that's allowed us (all but forced us, for our own good, really) to hold a mirror up to ourselves and see the truth about how we handle money. Many of them happen to be fabulously witty, and they've even made it possible to laugh at ourselves a bit . . . which makes any lesson easier to absorb.

But don't think about the famously droll and dry Ben Stein in *Ferris Bueller's Day Off* as emblematic of behavioral economists. ("Bueller? Bueller?") Who can resist snorting with laughter at the thought?! And to think he became a comedian to make fun of his boring economic self. Not to mention, movie director John Hughes recognized him for the rather accomplished speechwriter and commentator on politics and economics that he was! No, these behavioral economists are funny, entertaining, quirky, and definitely intellectually curious. Which is probably why they tend to be so good at connecting dots and seeming to predict the future and probe into how we humans will respond to their ideas. They are always looking at things and asking, "Why?" You name it, they are thinking about it. Why do we buy a certain toilet paper? Sure. Baseball decision-making? Yep. How long does it take to master a particular hobby or skill? Why not? NFL draft outcomes? Clearly. Why do we choose the health care we do? Been there.

Why do we refuse to floss our teeth twice a day when we know it's good for us and will save us money in the long run? You bet. Why do we make bad investment decisions? Done that. Behavioral economists are a fascinating breed who look at everyday conundrums and issues, try to make sense of them, and attempt to explain why we make the decisions we do. No matter how wayward or errant.

This isn't Robert Frost here—they're not taking the road less traveled—nor Jason Aldean and "swerving on a dirt road." Nope. These men and women are doing incredibly important and fascinating work to understand and shape the decisions we make every single day that impact our happiness, health, and financial security. These behavioral economists are trying to determine why human beings, while capable of brilliance, don't make optimal decisions. They spend an enormous amount of time thinking about the future, thinking about public policy, thinking about what changes in policy are going to have a positive impact for the greater good. They are sitting at the intersection of corporate America, academia, public policy, money, and psychology and, as businesspeople, we would be well served to pay attention to them.

I have had the privilege to work with and meet many of this bunch. Almost to a person they are energetic, engaging, practical, compassionate, and interested in helping others help themselves. Many of them are highly philanthropic, turning their energies to solving problems like poverty (Northwestern's Dean Karlan), to running think tanks focused on helping states run more efficiently (Arthur Laffer). They're often renaissance men and women who are ultimately curious about everything, writing screenplays and thrillers in their spare time (Charles Wheelan) or preparing for myriad TED Talks (Dan Ariely). You definitely want this group at your dinner party. They are unique, intellectually curious hybrids who understand the big picture and the details of mathematics and statistics. And on the whole, they are a very international lot who bring a broad global and cultural perspective to this exciting field. We can all be enriched at some level personally and professionally by hearing what they have to say. This cohort makes a real difference, and their impact in improving the lives of everyday Americans simply cannot not be underestimated.

Behaviors that make or break financial wellness

When it comes to health, financial, and emotional well-being decision-making, the following are some of the most important and recognizable behaviors. There are countless other behaviors (some of them overlapping or with very similar names) out there for you to explore, but here are examples of behaviors that I would argue are the most relevant in the context of the employer-employee relationship and financial wellness solutions at work.

If you look around, you might see them characterized a little differently, but spend any amount of time skimming the surface and you will start to get the idea.

- **Decision paralysis**—This is clearly manifested when employees are presented 401(k) investment options or a menu of more than one or two health insurance options. When you give people too many options, they tend to freeze up and will make no decision at all. Give them just a few options and help them understand the distinctions between them, and they are much more apt to make a decision and do so with some degree of confidence.

- **Default bias**—People tend to avoid complex decisions and tend to favor the easiest option. Default options remove some of the cognitive burden of making decisions and tell us what we're supposed to do. (Hint: That is why we provide simple automatic enrollment, automatic escalation, and asset diversification. That is why we prepay via payroll for health insurance, HSAs, and other things we need. This encourages a certain behavior. Without it, nobody would participate. They would keep meaning to do it and never get around to it. A default option at least gets us out of our own way by making an initial decision for us, even if it's not a perfect decision.)

- **Goal gradient theory**—People will work harder to achieve a goal as that goal gets closer. You know that 5k you signed up for five month ago? Well, it's now a month away, and I bet you suddenly are very focused on training. Retirement savings is a great example of this theory at work. The older people get, the more real retirement becomes, and the more they focus on it. (It also helps to explain why Millennials tend to avoid the retirement conversation and instead focus on student loan debt, which is a current issue for them. They're walking along the goal gradient at that point, and retirement looks like it's a hundred years away . . . until it isn't.)

- **Herding**—People tend to do what others are doing. We will do it without realizing it and without using our own information to make decisions for ourselves. It's not uncommon to hear herding discussed in conjunction with stock market bubbles or mass flocking to certain consumer goods for a certain period of time. One could argue that the student loan debt problem faced by Millennials is an example of herding. People chose to take on debt because they saw others doing it and thought it was the right thing to do, without necessarily pausing to examine if they could choose less-costly options, such as community college or trade school, or if they might feasibly be able to skip college altogether.

- **Gamification**—Humans are wired to love games, competition, winning, and rewards. The fact is, people will play games if the only thing they get are points, badges, or even modest recognition. Money doesn't even have to be involved for gamification to work.

- **Lack of self-control**—Ah, one of the essential plights of humanity. We have a really hard time choosing between what's good for us over the long term and what's gratifying right now. This affects countless decisions we make, such as our ability to put away cash for savings and leave it untouched.

- **Mental accounting**—This idea is often attributed to the work of Richard Thaler. People tend to treat money differently depending on its use, its source, and whether they feel like they got a good deal on something. This is in contrast to a formal accounting mentality, where we would theoretically focus more on the bottom-line outcomes of our choices. This can cause us to lose sight of the big picture quite quickly and make some very irrational decisions with money and investments. So, for example, we might view money we spend on everyday needs as distinct and unrelated to our total net worth.

- **Overconfidence**—I am the best driver on the road, right? Everyone believes they are right and above average. Someone who is unskilled at something will often tend to overestimate their own abilities. The legendary behavioral economist Daniel Kahnemann once told an interviewer that if he could eliminate one human bias, it would be this one.[4] This can play out in multiple ways. One example might be an employee who thinks they can handle their own financial planning and be stubborn about listening to outside advice. I recently was listening to a talk show hosted by one of the nation's leading consumer advocates. A woman called in, begging for advice on how to get her husband to hire a financial advisor. When the host asked her why he refused to hire help, she said, "He thinks he knows what he's doing. But he doesn't. And I think it's really hurting us." Clearly a case of dangerous overconfidence.

- **Pain of paying**—Some uses of money just seem more painful than others. For instance, it might feel much more painful to purchase a new furnace or a new roof than a new car. Or setting aside money for savings may feel painful because we feel the sting of short-term denial. This is why people avoid saving or making the sacrifices needed to pay off debt. Anything employers can do to help reduce that sense of pain will help employees help themselves in prioritizing how they use money.

- **Reciprocity**—People tend to respond to a gesture by providing something in return. This creates a virtuous cycle of reinforcement and can even tighten the bond between the two parties. Matching contributions to a 401(k) or matching employee giving to a charity are great examples of reciprocity in the context of the employer-employee relationship.

- **Reward substitution**—This is the phenomenon by which immediate rewards can be used to appeal to our more impulsive side that loves immediate gratification, to encourage us to undertake and sustain behaviors that are good for us in the long run.

- **Sunk cost effect**—Once we put money toward a particular choice or path, we can be prone to dig in and become even more committed to that choice, even if it isn't always the best one. My dad used to call this "throwing good money after bad." Say you bought a concert ticket in another city, only to find the cost to fly to that city has skyrocketed. You still might spend the money on the airfare rather than just try to sell the ticket to someone at a loss or just let it go. Or you might choose a terrible investment but continue to ride it to the bottom because you're already invested and don't want to give up. I've been on both sides of this equation, and this is one that often takes an expert and some very clear explanation of math to convince people to change course.

Behavioral economics at work in our everyday lives: the now-famous "nudge"

If you read the works of Professor Charles Wheelan (*Naked Economics, Naked Statistics*) or the books of Professor Dan Ariely (*Misbehaving, Irrationality*, and others) there is a common theme among all of them. Left to our devices (and based on a mountain of data), individuals make pretty bad decisions—decisions one can only hope we would not make if we had complete information, unlimited cognitive abilities, and complete self-control. Does that sound like anyone we know? Yea, no.

But what we do tend to respond well to is "the nudge." Thaler, who together with fellow writer Cass Sunstein made the idea of the nudge widespread, believes that "choice architecture" can help nudge us away from bad decisions and harmful biases toward choices that are ultimately better for ourselves, our families, and society.[5] This nudge phenomenon is precisely why auto-enrollment in 401(k) plans, while viewed by some as overly paternal and intrusive, work wonders in improving participation rates.

The nudge works, and it's one of the greatest gifts given to us by the field of behavioral economics.

What is a nudge and how do nudges help us make better decisions that help us realize better outcomes? A nudge, as behavioral economics use the term, is any aspect of the choice architecture that alters people's behavior in a predictable way without forbidding any options or significantly changing their economic incentives. As Thaler articulates, to count as a nudge, the intervention must be easy and cheap to avoid. Nudges are not mandates. Putting fruit at eye level is a nudge; banning candy is not. Nudges have and will continue to transform financial wellness outcomes through the design modifications that have been implemented in 401(k) plans. These benefit design modifications came directly from the work of Richard Thaler, Shlomo Benartzi and, more recently, Lesley Turner and Dean Karlan, among others. These transformative adjustments to various programs and financial solutions are a direct result of their collective thinking.

Nudge is about choices—how we make them and how we're led to make better ones. Richard Thaler and Cass Sunstein offered a new perspective on how to prevent countless bad mistakes we make in our lives, including ill-advised investments, consumption of unhealthy foods, neglect of our natural resources, and other numerous bad decisions regarding health care, our families, education, and countless other areas of our lives. Citing decades of cutting-edge behavioral science research, they demonstrate that sensible "choice architecture" can successfully nudge people toward the best decision without restricting their freedom of choice. Terrifically straightforward, informative, and often very entertaining, their bestselling book, *Nudge*, is a must-read for anyone with an interest in our individual and collective well-being.

What employers can do with these insights. Whatever you do, I'd urge caution about dismissing behavioral economics as hype, pop psychology, or fluff. While you may not have the time or appetite to go deep into study, there are a few concrete things you can do to make sure your team is current on this field of study and how you might use it to improve your ability to attract and retain employees. Make it a topic during one of your committee meetings. Bring in a guest speaker. Your record keepers, investment consultants, and investment managers have amazing resources at their disposal. Just ask them.

Get acquainted with this area of study, which has guided employee benefits for almost forty years. Perhaps you studied behavioral economics in business school. And maybe it was called something different—organizational behavior, perhaps? That's great. Just bear in mind the field continues to evolve rapidly, and it's important to keep tabs on it so that you can apply the learnings within your own business strategy and operations.

Create a book club or study group with your colleagues and executives, fellow practitioners, even employees outside the HR function. This can be a fun way to expose your team to some of the leading thinkers discussed in this book, and virtually all of their more well-known books have information that can be of help to any of us in understanding ourselves and others and the interesting behaviors we humans exhibit when it comes to money. Be sure to take a look at "Recommended Reading" in the Appendix for a number of ideas.

Look at your current benefits lineup to see how they do or don't make use of behavioral economics. This is a really fun exercise. It's the first time many realize that the tax deductibility of 401(k) plans makes it easy to take advantage of. The matching contributions make it almost impossible to not participate, and the automatic enrollment does actually make it impossible not to participate! Hmm, wonder where those ideas came from?

Consider adding behavioral economics tidbits to your employee education efforts. Understanding why people act the way they do and why they make the decisions they make is important in order to offer the right benefits, with the right features, with the real potential to help employees achieve the "preferred" outcome relative to their financial wellness.

By making sure you and your teams are armed with some basics, and layering this together with basic demographic insights, you can develop a broader context and a stronger basis for decision-making. You can use this information to craft a benefits lineup that accounts for the realities of human nature, creates more positive financial behaviors, and improves both the individual and the business. We all need nudges and incentives—and, yes, physical or virtual rewards and recognition—when we do things that we may not ordinarily do. Were we walking 10,000 steps a day before Fitbit? I didn't think so. The same idea explains why apps like Acorns are both effective and important. They use smaller, more incremental savings strategies for those with less means and less available income to take smaller, more manageable steps toward financial wellness. Together, the seemingly small solutions like these are the ones that are going to help us tackle the biggest problems. After all, how do you eat an elephant? One bite at a time.

BEHAVIOR NUDGES

Reward Substitution

Immediate rewards, which appeal to people's impulsive nature, can encourage behaviors that are actually good in the long run. Employers should look for ways to embed reward substitution in their benefits programs, such as a cash incentive for wellness checks or other steps toward their health or financial wellbeing.

If you want to be an employer who's ready for the future, watch the behavioral economists. Trust me, they are like the smartest, friendliest kid in the hardest math class you ever had. They'll show you where the ball is heading and help you be ready for what's next and keep a pulse on Millennials as their behaviors toward money continue to evolve.

Questions to consider

- Do we realize just how much influence behavioral economists have had on how workplace benefits are designed (e.g., automatic payroll deduction, company matching, program rewards and incentives)?

- What can we learn from this academic research?

- How can we help nudge our employee base to make better financial decisions? How can we better help them help themselves?

- Are we integrating gamification, rewards, and encouragement to drive better uptake of certain benefits?

- In what ways are we seeing some of the principles of behavioral economics playing out in how our employees choose and use the benefits we offer?

- How are we keeping a pulse on the latest developments in behavioral economics?

- Have we ever discussed this as a team, or have we ever considered doing something like a book club that looks at some of the many books written by leading social scientists, organizational behaviorists, and behavioral economists?

9

THE GROWTH OF CONSUMERISM: GLORY DAYS FOR EMPLOYEES, NEW OPPORTUNITIES FOR EMPLOYERS

"What consumerism really is, at its worst, is getting people to buy things that don't actually improve their lives."

—Jeff Bezos, Executive Chairman, Amazon

Definitions of the term "consumerism" vary widely. You can find far-ranging definitions that reference everything from the complexities of Keynesian economic theory to psychology-based definitions that speak to why we humans are wired to think that buying things can make us happy (temporarily at least).

For the purpose of this discussion, let's consider a very simple definition of consumerism: *the products and services consumers prefer, the features consumers prefer those products and services to have, and how consumers prefer to have those products and services delivered.*

Let's also consider that more than 90 percent of Americans now have an internet connection at home, and more than 96 percent of Americans now have a cell phone of some sort. And lest we forget, more people own a mobile device on this planet than a toothbrush. Maybe there's a market opportunity. And in March 2020, *Forbes* reported that COVID had driven a 35–85 percent increase in the use of fintech apps, up by more than 70 percent,[1] the very types of apps we discussed previously. In 2018 and 2019, the U.S. was second only to China in retail e-commerce sales. We're firmly in an era where consumers in all adult age groups from around the world have become uber consumers: they want what they want, when they want it, and they expect virtually every company they interact with in every part of their lives to be able to meet that demand.

A quick look at some other statistics give us an even deeper sense of the evolved consumer.

- Ninety-six percent of U.S. adults own a cell phone.

- Seventy-three percent of consumers want self-service technology.

- Only 38 percent of consumers actually want to talk with a human when engaging with a brand.

- In the United States, people spend two hours and three minutes on social media each day.

- Telehealth usage is expected to grow sevenfold by 2025, a compound annual growth rate of close to 40 percent.

In the age of Amazon, Zappos, Zoom, DoorDash, Esurance, DocuSign, Carvana, and countless other consumer-first, born-digital companies, we've all become incredibly demanding consumers. It's like Sally in *When Harry Met Sally*, driving waiters mad with her ultra-picky instructions, or me ordering dinner when I'm out, which usually starts with "unless you want to see my face blow up like Hitch's, *please* no onions nor anything related to the onion family." (If you know the classic *When Harry Met Sally*, can you imagine her giving her usual litany of instructions on her UberEats or DoorDash order?!) Whether we're conscious of it or not, we now want experiences in every part of our life to meet multiple numerous criteria:

- Digital and mobile—serve me on the device of my choosing, whether it's my laptop, tablet, or smartphone.

- Simple—make it easy to compare, buy, use, and troubleshoot your product or service, and don't make me sign in more than once to get everything I need.

- Personalized—prove to me that you know me and that I'm more than a number to you.

- Always available—I don't operate on a nine-to-five schedule; neither should your company.

- Self-service—I want to be able to find what I need and conduct my business on my own, so make that easy for me.

- Relevant—offer me products and services that matter to me.

- Fun—make it engaging and interesting for me. I have a short attention span and little free time.

- Seamless and channel-less—I don't know or care about you "channels," I just want it to be easy to interact with your company, however I choose to do that.

The Rise of E-Commerce in the United States
E-Commerce sales as a percentage of total retail sales in the United States*

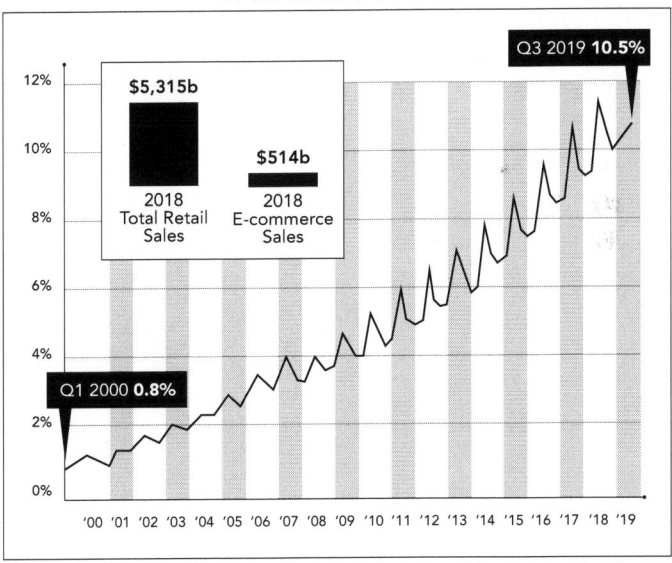

*not seasonally adjusted

In simplest terms, employers should care about the permanent and sustained growth in e-commerce because employees are voracious consumers. They expect employers to deliver outstanding online experiences and tools that are clear, easy to use, and help them make informed choices. This extends to "shopping" at work for financial wellness benefits.

But why should employers care?

Because employees are consumers first, they've come to expect these types of consumer-first services and experiences from their employers as well, in everything from recruiting to onboarding to payroll to benefits selection and delivery. As we've examined at multiple points in this book, we have talked about how companies, HR, and senior management recognize that their employees are the company's first and most important customers. Companies that recognize how critical it is to have a pragmatic empathy with employees—one that recognizes that employees are humans first, consumers second, and employees third—are the ones that will be the most successful and that understanding, empathy, and relatability is critical to hiring and attracting the workforce of the future.

Employers that embrace their employees as the new consumer and offer products and services they expect, delivered in the way they expect them, are the employers that stand the greatest chance of winning the war of talent hiring and retention.

It is amazing to witness the sea change happening in corporate America. The antiquated ways in which employees were once treated or offered benefits or opportunities looks and feels like it's from another planet or at least from the 1980s. Today I can order my groceries and dinner while confirming a weekend trip with my daughters, book tickets to Country Thunder, reschedule a workout, and talk to my mom on the phone, all while in the back of an Uber. Which, by the way, I did the other day.

The collapsing wall between personal experience and employee experience

Even prior to COVID, the lines between our personal experiences as consumers and our employee experiences were beginning to blur more and more. We could, at 6 a.m. or midnight on any sleepless night, be on our laptop shopping for a new SUV and car insurance, while logging in to Workday or ADP to check our payroll tax withholding and health plan selection, while waiting for a doc to join our mobile phone app for a quick telemedicine visit about that earache that just won't go away on its own. COVID and the new world of remote work has only blurred those lines even further, and they'll never be redrawn as they once were. When you combine this reality, the ever-expanding role of the employer as life mentor/coach and prime source of wellness solutions, and what we've come to understand about the expectations placed on employers by powerful demographic segments such as Millennials, we see that Yogi Berra was spot-on when he cheekily said, "The future ain't what it used to be!"

Mercer, a leading provider of benefits, describes us as living in the age of Consumerism 4.0, or the Fourth Industrial Revolution, in which the 4.0 employee-as-consumer expects "on-demand access, personalization, actionable insights, reference/peer-based reviews, and more." Mercer adds that, "Employers need to design and deliver strategies that support this new experience to improve the value from their health and benefits investments."

Some of this is manifested in the career development aspects of the employers' role. It's a mentor, life coach, physical, emotional, and financial relationship that provides more than just annual reviews of a thumbs-up or thumbs-down nature. Millennials want constant feedback, nurturing, and guidance. For better or worse, they are the generation of the participation trophy. You're a winner just for showing up. After all, as Woody Allen said, 90 percent of life is showing up. Yogi Berra had a plethora of insights that were made for 2021 America. "If you don't know where you're going, you'll end up someplace else. Baseball is 90 percent mental and the other half is physical. When you come to a fork in the road, take it. If the world were perfect, it wouldn't be." The world is a better place today because Yogi was in it. And I'm a Cubs fan.

In short, the way in which employees buy financial services, insurance, pay bills, balance their budgets, pay their mortgage, and consume their benefits must be as modern and seamless *within* the work setting as it is in their everyday life outside work. Your employees expect the same customer experience with your company that they have in their everyday lives. As employers, your most important customers are your employees. And even more noteworthy, as we'll explore below, generations of incoming employees, especially Millennials—

view themselves not so much as your employee or a unit of human capital, but as a customer or client of your company, with you competing for their time and attention just like every other company with which they interact.

The colorful history and inevitable future of consumerism

Long before founding Sheridan Road Financial, I was a technology investment banker working obscene and ridiculous hours and sometimes, more often than I would like to admit, sleeping under my desk. I grew up reading *Liar's Poker*, by Michael Lewis, and lived through what my DLJ Associate classmate, Peter Troob, recounted in his book, *Monkey Business—Swinging Through the Wall Street Jungle*. My twenties are a blur, a mixture of all-night war-room sessions and weekly flights from city to city helping to take all sorts of software, technology services, and internet companies public. And, I might also mention, perhaps a few too many Royales with Cheese.

I remember having a conversation with my college classmate and friend Jon Callaghan, Founder of True Ventures, in my Chicago apartment in the summer of 1995, about eyeballs, cookies, AI, prescriptive and all things e-commerce. And I was still using dial-up US Robotics modems to get onto the world wide web. I had trouble tracking his now-clairvoyant mumbo jumbo, as he was at the vanguard of investments in an array of internet search engines, data hosting, managed services, data analytics, digital marketing, and messaging companies—that I would actually come to take public or sell just a few short years later. It turns out, he was part of an internet incubator that invested in and helped created internet search engines, digital marketing, and messaging companies such as Alta Vista, Lycos, GeoCities, and Navisite. These companies, in what now is referred to as Internet Version 1.0, helped create the technology foundation well before Google was a gleam in anyone's eye.

As a matter of fact, during a meeting with the then-small, fledgling search engine with twenty-eight people and a funny name, this group of seemingly high schoolers proselytized about their name being used as a verb. At that very moment, I had the audacity to proclaim that search was over. The victors had conquered this last frontier. After all, hadn't they heard of Yahoo! As I sung that catchy phrase, I could see the color fall from my colleagues faces, the meeting wrapped up quickly, and Google's Larry Page never returned my future calls. I subsequently convinced myself that you win some and you lose some. But given I am still talking about it to this day, it's fair to say that was a big whiff. I mean big. Interestingly, while perhaps the Bay Area was ready, the rest of the world wasn't quite ready for these companies at that time. But without Internet Version 1.0, we wouldn't be where we are today in an era of creativity, technology advancement, and UX (user experience) innovation that unquestionably forms the bedrock of the modern technology landscape.

The point is, for more than twenty-five years, we've been moving toward the current era of digital consumerism. After all, consider visionaries like Bill Gates and Steve Jobs, and the early venture capitalists who believed in them. They foresaw 2021 decades ago. Things moved slowly at first, as companies you've never heard of before, like IRI spin-off VideoCart, Ask Jeeves, CMGI, Internet Capital Group, Divine Interventures, Beatnik (Thomas Dolby's startup and precursor to Apple Music), MySpace (the infamous precursor to Facebook), and Peapod and Webvan (the earliest grocery delivery companies) tried to break through, either hobbling along or flopping, often to be reborn in newer and better forms, with more advanced bandwidth, Wi-Fi, mobile devices, and yes, consumers. These were ingenious ideas that were just ahead of their time. They tried to combine emerging technology, early behavioral economics, and online adoption, but neither the technology nor the consumer were quite ready for them. Now the technology is here, the ability to scale is here, consumers are ready, and the most innovative employers have recognized the need to offer consumer-like experiences to employees at every stage of their employment journey. This underlying vision of the future, powered by the ideas of AI, advanced data analytics, and other tech enablers, has been the vision of the future for decades. The difference is that it's only now that the ecosystem is ready. After all, just look at the vision and writings of Bill Gates, Steve Jobs, and the venture capitalists who staked them. They envisioned today decades ago. Let's go explore this new world.

Consumerism at work: examples abound

One doesn't have to look far to see living examples of how consumerism has infiltrated the American workplace. Take open enrollment as one of the most obvious examples. Even as recently as five or ten years ago, the process was cumbersome and annoyingly paper intensive. Employers might host a series of calls or in-person meetings, offer a few printed packets or PDFs explaining benefits, and employees would have to often rely on water-cooler conversations with each other to figure things out. And half the time, employees weren't confident in their selections but didn't have the time or patience to sit through one more mind-numbing benefits meeting with the 401(k) or HR rep. Individuals spend ninety seconds selecting investments in their 401k plan–sixty seconds on the actual asset managers, and thirty seconds making sure it adds up to 100 percent. Four plus eight, carry the one . . .

Fast-forward to the current day, and some of the nation's largest companies are using fun, interactive, digital tools like Jellyvision's "ALEX" to help employees make all kinds of decisions about how to choose and use workplace benefits. Amanda Lannert, the CEO of Jellyvision, is an

BEHAVIOR NUDGES

Gamification

People like to play games and they will go to great lengths playing even if all they get are points. Can student debt payments be turned into a game or competition?

early adopter of how best to deliver solutions through the employer. It's no surprise that Jellyvision was spawned from a company that initially focused on educational media and video games. Jellyvision describes itself as "an award-winning technology company whose interactive software talks people through important, complex, and potentially snooze-inducing life decisions—like choosing a health-care insurance plan, saving for retirement, or navigating a leave of absence—in simple, fun, and engaging ways. The company explains what makes them unique: "Our recipe: behavioral science, purposeful humor, mighty tech, and oregano. Our SaaS [software as a service] employee communication platform ALEX is used by more than 1,500 companies with more than 18 million employees in total—including 114 of the Fortune 500 and two-fifths of the country's twenty-five largest companies. ALEX helps employees at these companies, whose health insurance premiums total more than $115 billion, make better decisions about their insurance plan options, 401(k) allocations, and financial wellness." And once employees get a taste of these types of tools and experiences, they expect them in every part of their lives. I worked and brainstormed with Amanda Lannert to figure out how to deliver the same type of benefit to employees around their financial wellness and retirement needs. Creative and curious and always looking at how to make an impact, Amanda is an early mover of solution delivery through the employer.

Employee intranet sites offer another highly visible example of consumer culture in the workplace. While not all companies agree about the need for an intranet or how much to invest in them, the fact is that corporate intranets have evolved greatly from their original form. Once boring link farms that were organized around company structure rather than employee needs, had no visual interest, and were created with absolutely no consideration of UX design, many of them are now highly visual, modular, personalized infomarts that deliver rich online experiences and engaging content that rival any consumer-facing website—all designed around employee needs and how they think of the world of work and what they need to accomplish their job, learn the latest company news, or manage their benefits.

Millennials: a driving force for an increasingly consumer-centric workplace experience

Even before Millennials hit the workforce, many employers were beginning to offer more consumer-like experiences to employees. But Millennials, the first digital natives and notoriously demanding consumers, have forced consumerism through the front doors of the workplace once and for all.

They've grown up in a seamless, mobile, on-demand personalized world, and they expect employers to behave like all other businesses and provide those same sorts of experiences in order to be seen as worthy. When you combine this with the Millennials' pervasive expectation that the employer be their primary provider of financial stability and advice, it makes the need for employers to provide best-in-class financial wellness benefits, delivered in the way Millennials expect them to be delivered, an absolute imperative rather than a nice-to-have option. Millennials want easy, intuitive, engaging user experiences and, at the end of the day, if you have a benefits provider who provides a clunky or confusing experience, they don't blame the third-party provider, they blame you.

And part of what makes them an even more powerful force are things like their no-holds-barred style of transparency and innate ability to weaponize information on social platforms like Facebook, Instagram, Twitter, LinkedIn, or Glassdoor. If they have a bumpy onboarding experience, a confusing or annoying experience enrolling in benefits, or find out their friends are getting a financial wellness benefit you're not offering, they won't hesitate to go on their industry networking group on Facebook and tell literally thousands of people about it. Nor will they hesitate to call out an employer brand unapologetically to their one-thousand followers on Glassdoor. For example, just recently a colleague told me that in a large metro area networking group (the majority of whom are Millennials), a question was posed about unlimited PTO (paid time off). The question elicited hundreds of responses, the majority of them torching current or former employers and saying it was merely a way for employers to try and get out of paying unpaid leave. That same week, another person posed a question about student loans, and one post on the topic elicited dozens of comments comparing employers that did or did not offer student loan debt relief.

They can also be highly critical of employers and their environmental and social responsibility efforts. A 2019 *Fast Company* survey of one-thousand employees showed that 40 percent of Millennials have at some point chosen a job because of what they view as the company's sustainability. (According to the study, 25 percent of Gen Xers and 17 percent of Baby Boomers report using this same decision filter.) This study was in line with many similar previous studies and only serves to reinforce the discerning consumer mindset that now dominates among prospective and current employees.[2]

My good friend Dr. Richard Chaifetz, the Founder and CEO of ComPsych, the world's largest provider of employee assistance programs (EAPs), sees this convergence of technology, the mandate for workplace wellness, and the rise of critical consumerism at work as a powerful opportunity for both employees and employers. His company has grown rapidly to offer services that "help people navigate the broad spectrum of life issues," ranging from traditional EAP programs to financial guidance from highly trained experts such as CPAs and CFPs to help employees manage the financial stressors that affect their emotional health and work productivity. He says, "It's an incredible opportunity to provide meaningful benefits that employees need in a way that works for them, whether it's self-service or mediated by a human support representative or enhanced with AI." He adds, "It's an incredible time to be able to offer benefits that can truly make a difference in the quality of life and productivity of an employee."

He adds one more important point, and that's regarding employee privacy. While Millennials are almost notorious for their disregard for privacy and their radical transparency, employers and their providers will have to balance this consumer preference they demonstrate with consumer and workplace privacy laws to ensure they're operating in a way that's in sync with various laws. The landscape continues to change in this regard and employers will need to continue to look to their benefits consultants and provider partners to steer them properly, and to also be sensitive to employee sentiments regarding privacy of personal information.

What this consumer culture means for employers

Just as employers need not be experts in demographics or behavioral economics, you need not immerse yourself in modern trends in consumerism. Instead, it is important that key members of your benefits leadership team keep a pulse on key consumer trends, together with other top-line trends in demographics, in order to make strategic decisions regarding your financial wellness benefits for employees. The call to action here is twofold:

1. Bear in mind that employees are consumers first, and consumers expect the same purchasing and customer service experience inside the confines of their employer as outside their employer; and,

2. The more your benefits team can offer integrated, channel-agnostic solutions that help employees address their most pressing financial concerns, the more you can increase your employer brand equity with an ever-more discerning workforce of consumers.

We are not just a nation of consumers, we're a world of consumers. In countries all over the world, retail e-commerce only continues to rise. In India, e-commerce sales rose a whopping 30 percent between 2018 and 2019 alone. This means if you have a global workforce and not just a U.S.-based one, all the more reason to pay attention.

Perhaps you never imagined there'd ever be such a thing as a robo-advisor for investing, or maybe you'd never use it yourself. Or, if you're like me, you may be forced to admit you never dreamed Amazon would explode as it has, or just how effective they would be at convincing us to buy more and more things with their incredibly powerful suggestive purchasing techniques (developed, by the way, by brilliant behavioral economists!). While I've had the pleasure of working with a lot of very innovative executives, I've also talked to countless executives who never believed that Amazon would be so omnipresent in our lives, or that consumers would be willing to give up an extraordinary amount of privacy in return for digital access and convenience. We all know someone who has said, "No, no, no, that'll never happen!" while we, as consumers, are in the midst of and taking part in that very transformation ourselves. During business school at Kellogg, we all laughed when we reviewed the case study of Polaroid or Kodak or Blockbuster, for either failing to see what was happening around them or being able to leverage their installed base to their benefit. Well, here we go again. What fifty- or one-hundred-year-old companies are not going to improvise and realize that the world has changed forever? They will go the way of Blockbuster.

The fact is, we're living in an age of nearly unfettered consumerism. The future is here and your current and future employees—who are consumers as much as anything else—want and expect contemporary, consumer-friendly solutions from you, their employers. Regardless of how preferences may change over time, what matters most is to simply be aware of where the world is and where it's headed when it comes to consumer preferences. Don't stick your head in the sand. Be alert for opportunities to appeal to the inner consumer that's inside of every single one of your employees.

While this might sound daunting, it presents a glorious opportunity for employers and for those of us who develop financial wellness benefits for employees. It's a perfect moment for a more purposeful, prescriptive approach to financial wellness. It means we can take these things that we know about human behavior and consumer preferences and appetite for a more sophisticated employee experience, and begin to take the upper hand in the battle for financial wellness and actually help our employees improve their life outcomes. We can exploit this knowledge for good and use it to take the high road and offer employees a mix of financial wellness benefits they can understand and actually use to solve some of the toughest pressures they face. What if, rather than encouraging people to take on more debt, or manipulating someone to buy that avocado slicer that will just sit in a drawer creating buyer's remorse, we can instead play a role in offering meaningful solutions that improve the financial betterment for our employees? Now that is a trend I think we can all get behind.

Questions to consider

- Are we treating employees like consumers or clients with particular needs and preferences?

- Do our current offerings, as well as our rollouts, delivery, and ongoing support, reflect the same seamless, frictionless convenience our employees experience when purchasing goods and services in the "outside" world?

- Are we meeting the demands of our employees in terms of how they want to interact with our business and the benefits we offer?

- Do we have an intranet where these consumers can evaluate options and make decisions on their benefits, retirement, investments, HSA, and financial wellness?

10

THE RISE OF TECHNOLOGY AND BIG DATA: WHAT IT MEANS FOR FINANCIAL WELLNESS

"The most valuable commodity I know of is information."

—Gordon Gekko, *Wall Street*

There've been a handful of times in my life when I recognized that the world was moving at a breakneck pace and would never be the same.

The first time the realization hit me was in high school AP BC calculus with Mr. Hammond. It was a small class, maybe fifteen of us. There was nowhere to hide. On this particular day, I was absolutely lost on the linear calculus proofs Mr. Hammond was discussing.

Now, you should know that in high school, I played sports, was president of the Spanish Club, and wrote for the creative writing magazine (cleverly named *The Wit.*). I even took C++ and Cobol programming, but all it got me was an ulcer, a trip to the eye doctor, and migraines. I was one of the few in class who wasn't on the math team or computer team or in the science club.

(Think Anthony Michael Hall in *The Breakfast Club*.) One day in class I gazed over at Brian Jacobson, one of my affectionately nerdy classmates who was not only not paying attention to the proofs on the board but appeared to be programming a video game on his Commodore 64 under his desk. I swear, to this day, he created Asteroids but never got credit for it. Basically, my classmates were geeking out in perfect harmony with Mr. Hammond, while I was trying to figure out how to sharpen

> **Defining terms for this chapter:**
>
> **Fintech**—According to Investopedia, it's "new tech that seeks to improve and automate the delivery and use of financial services. At its core, fintech is utilized to help companies, business owners and consumers better manage their financial operations, processes, and lives by utilizing specialized software and algorithms that are used on computers and, increasingly, smartphones."
>
> Source: https://www.investopedia.com/terms/f/fintech.asp
>
> **Big data**—According to SAS, one of the world's leading technology firms, "Big data is a term that describes the large volume of data – both structured and unstructured – that inundates a business on a day-to-day basis. But it's not the amount of data that's important. It's what organizations do with the data that matters. Big data can be analyzed for insights that lead to better decisions and strategic business moves."

my pencil without a pencil sharpener. I felt like Wally Cleaver and an early hominid who had just seen fire for the first time.

I knew I was out of my league. I knew there were humans who were going to create amazing things that I would never understand how to fully use, much less create myself.

Years after that calculus class, I moved on to my first job in investment banking, literally on Wall Street, equipped with a then-state-of-the-art pager and Lotus Notes. I'd get paged by my boss and have to duck into an office or store and use a landline to check in. Next came the PDA (personal digital assistant) with a stylus, the Palm Pilot. And then, nirvana. In the form of a Blackberry.

On January 9, 2007, Steve Jobs introduced to the world a strange and alluring device, something that "combined three products: a revolutionary mobile phone, a widescreen iPod with touch controls, and a breakthrough internet communications device with desktop-class email, web browsing, searching, and maps—into one small and lightweight handheld device."

The gadgets were great, but this seminal event marked the second time I knew the world had turned a corner into the future of technology.

And at the time, I think the only benefit my employer offered was a one-size-fits-all medical insurance plan and a 401(k) with so many investment options it made my head spin.

Technology, devices, consumers—as well as employers and workplace benefits—have been hurtling into the future together ever since. But not always at an even pace. Sometimes ideas and technology weren't aligned with the infrastructure or bandwidth to handle them. Sometimes products were ready, but consumers weren't. Sometimes fintech vendors wanted access to employees through employers, but employers were skeptical or simply not ready. But at some point in recent history, the stars aligned. Technology, consumer need, and business were in the exact same spot at the exact same moment.

Why this is relevant for employers

Today we sit at a pivotal moment in history and society. We're at a point when technology (especially financial technology or "fintech") data analytics, and consumer-employee needs and wants intersect almost completely, and employers sit squarely in the middle with the unprecedented power to complete that connection. For any product or technology to take hold, there has to be the product capability, an addressable market or need, and a frictionless distribution channel. We're there. We have fintech companies delivering an array of financial wellness solutions, employees raised as digital natives (i.e., Millennials), who desperately need and want them, and employers who are finally technologically ready and beginning to recognize how they can help employees by giving them access to these always-on, digital-first, mobile-always financial wellness solutions.

By far, the biggest segment of investment for venture capital and private equity over the last five years has been fintech. Its proliferation means financial solutions can be deployed to consumers faster and more cost effectively than ever before. And with U.S. employers naturally having

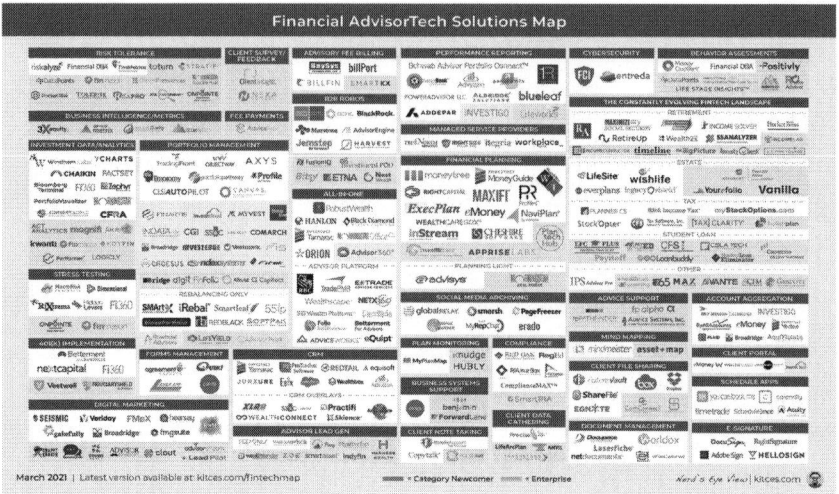

The fintech world moves fast and changes constantly. Trying to create a current chart of fintech brands is like trying to chart the wind. What is constant, however, is the growth of fintech brands are catering to the financial wellness needs of employees. These innovators are finding distribution channels with employers who understand the value of giving employees digital tools designed to help improve financial wellness.

access to millions of consumers at scale and having cloud-based payroll platforms now widely in place across industries and segments, from microbusinesses to conglomerates, they're a logical channel for the plug-n-play delivery of the fintech solutions that can help consumers (a.k.a. employees) the most—solutions like loan repayment, student loan solutions, investment advisory, mortgage shopping, and emergency savings accumulation, to name just a few. Add to this the rise of big data and BI (business intelligence), employers and their benefits vendor partners can now understand, target, and anticipate employees and their needs with an unprecedented level of accuracy and insight. Propelled by savvy fintech leaders and innovative employers, technology and analytics are now being combined to open a new world of mutually beneficial possibilities for the targeted delivery of digital financial wellness solutions for employees. Employers who take the time to understand the basics of the fintech landscape, as well as the power of big data and what it can tell us—and find practical ways to harness both together for the benefit of their business and their workforce—are the ones who will create the most resilient businesses, the most financially resilient workforce, and be best positioned to offer well-targeted, technology-driven financial wellness solutions that employees need and desire. And hence, be the best-positioned employer of choice.

Follow the money: venture capital investments in fintech

For forty years, venture capital (VC) investments in fintech have served as a bit of a crystal ball. The total flow of money to fintech creators is astonishing. By the end of the first quarter of 2020, the cumulative value of investments in the fintech industry reached $107.9 billion.[1] From 2017 to 2019, budgeting and financial planning solutions, just one category among many in fintech, grew by 20 percent.[2] VC tends to invest in things that seem crazy at the time, but then become staples in our society in ten years or less. Knowing where VCs are investing in terms of direct-to-consumer and employee financial wellness can help HR executives and influencers have a sense of what's coming and what's gaining steam. VCs are sort of like futurists. Not everything they support will come true or have staying power, but more often than not, they turn out to be pretty accurate. In fact, venture capitalists are like the kindred spirits of behavioral economists. They're toiling away, investing in things that they know will come to fruition in the next decade. If we watch what they're doing, they'll show us where the ball is going in terms of solutions that will be coming to market.

Harnessing the power and democratization of big data

It's surprising to me how few employers I talk to seem to be making use of data and big-data techniques to make decisions about their benefits, including financial wellness benefits. Sure, they might monitor some basic KPIs like 401(k) contribution levels or the number of hardship withdrawals, but there's more that most employers could be doing to make use of data on their own employees or outside data to do more effective benchmarking and strategic planning. Simple awareness or application can make a huge difference and impact in someone's life.

I understand that every company will be different in terms of the amount and quality of data they have, as well as the staff and tools they have to make sense of it. That's OK. You can take a crawl, walk, run approach to make use of the data you have in order to make more informed decisions about which financial wellness benefits to offer your employee base. Think about how important it is to have data or statistics on your customers or clients. Or how you track and monetize your new business opportunities. Salesforce has built itself into a behemoth in the customer relationship management (CRM) space—helping companies merely organize, strategize, and execute on sales pipelines. Obviously easier said than done; it's not just about the data, but putting it in a format and in a way that you can actually use it effectively. This is an area where your benefits partners and plan consultants can be a tremendous resource to you.

Yes, your employee base may be very unique. But at the same time, there are some very consistent and universally applicable patterns we can draw from, large data sets of employees with similar demographics to your own.

Jeff Faber of HUB International explains, "Enormous employers like the Fortune 50s of the world have massive data at their disposal, where they can see trends and implications even on low-frequency events. That's great. But you can take an employer of three-hundred lives or five-hundred lives, and still learn things from that data. You can also compare that to outside data, bump them together, and learn things from them that we didn't know before in terms of which financial wellness benefits to stop offering, start offering, or refine in their current form in order to improve employee uptake and outcomes."

The fact is, regardless of your industry, location, or size, big data has evolved to a point where we as financial and benefits experts can use big data concepts and apply it to smaller data sets. For instance, an employer might say, "That'll never happen here" about something like 401(k) withdrawals reaching alarming levels or employees being caught with absolutely no emergency funds. But what if it did? And if we could show you in the three or four markers or leading indicators pointing toward a certain scenario or situation ahead of it happening, then you might be able to react to it weeks or months earlier. Even in cases where an employer offers a fintech application to employees on a standalone basis without full-on integration, those applications can generate valuable anonymous data to get a sense of employee financial wellness in order to target particular problem areas and refine their benefits strategy to better meet the needs of the employee base.[3]

If you are in a smaller to mid-sized company and convinced you are lacking any useful sources of data, you may have more than you think. Your data resides primarily in three places: your payroll provider, your insurance carrier/insurance broker, and your 401k record keeper. There are also national, regional, and demographic databases to gain averages across health care and retirement.

There's also an interesting advantage that smaller employers can have in finding that sweet spot between data points and real insight into your employees. As colleagues like Andrea Goodkin, head of Total Rewards and Human Capital Consulting, and I talk with employers of all sizes, we see that a smaller employer can sometimes have interesting advantages over a much larger employer. Says Andrea, "In a smaller company, you and your managers can really get to know your people in a particularly deep way in terms of what they might be going through and what support they might need in order to improve their financial wellness. Marrying that information with the insight available through larger data sets can help you see your people in a much more human dimension (i.e., far beyond a mere set of data points you would be dealing with if you're a Fortune 50-type huge employer). This makes it much easier to take the right actions as an employer to support your people."

The fine line: ethical use of data

In making use of any data, each employer must bear in mind the ethical and legal issues involved, as well as employee preference and tolerance for privacy. Charlie Nelson, Chief Executive Officer, Retirement and Employee Benefits of Voya, reminds us that regulations and how employers and employees want to interact with data and fintech tools are not always on a perfectly even front with each other. He says, "It does create questions about comfort level, and how you use data to create a better experience for users. Employers and their fintech providers can aggregate data within reason in order to improve their offerings, while at the same time provide layers of privacy protections where required or wanted by the employer or the employee."

Nelson goes on to use a particularly interesting analogy about the natural tensions between what people want and need, what data we could get on employees if privacy and legality were no issue, and just how far technology and data analytics have come. "It's like we're trying to bring two magnets together and they're repelling one another to some degree," he explains. "One of them is technology and the fact that our capabilities are further ahead than our regulations. And the other magnet is our desire for privacy and our comfort levels with being willing to surrender some privacy in order to get access to targeted solutions we know would help us."

Richard Chaifetz, mentioned earlier, whose company has seen explosive growth, agrees we're living in very interesting times. "We have an entire generation of digital natives who grew up with social media, who have zero problems telling their deepest secrets to an online therapy group, and who prefer to schedule and get everything from addiction counseling to financial planning online from people they've never even met and who are storing all their most personal data somewhere in the cloud." He adds, "We all must operate within the various regulations that we have in industries like financial services, health insurance, and so on. It's an interesting challenge that we will have to navigate as we look for ways to match employer-sponsored benefits with workers and their needs, and as we try to keep the technology, the privacy regulations and concerns, and user appetite all moving at a somewhat even pace."

So you're not a VC tech or data expert: who to rely on for help

While big data and data analytics can be intimidating or boring, working with an expert who understands them and can make them useful to your business is the real key to putting it to good use.[4] This is where benefits experts can and should be your greatest resources. They have access to "big data" in the biggest sense of the word—enormous data sets for employee and consumer groups of all types and sizes together, years of trendline data, along with the machine learning and AI tools needed to run them through all kinds of retrospective analysis and forward-looking predictive modeling.

But in addition to the data and the tools, it's critical that your partners and consultants bring a powerful human element, deep experience, and differentiated thinking to the mix. It's the human expertise combined with the data and tools that can really give you the greatest edge in determining what kind of financial wellness offerings will be of the greatest benefit to your employees and to your business. I'll again refer to my friend and colleague Jeff Faber, who explains it best by saying, "It's not the wand, but the magician that matters" when it comes to solving challenges as complex as employee financial wellness.

Whether it's your retirement plan consultant, your insurance or EAP client manager, your HR or human capital consultants, don't be afraid to lean heavily on them. This is their job. They have decades and decades of experience with this; they should be looking far out on the horizon and should have a strong position to offer you on the subject of how you can and should be making the highest use of fintech and data—big *or* small.

Implications for employers

By no means do you have to become an expert in fintech or data analytics. But by lifting up out of everyday operations and making sure you are keeping some sort of pulse on fintech solutions that are growing or gaining traction among consumers, especially among generations of digital natives such as Millennials—and therefore may have some real staying power and utility for your employees—you can stay a step ahead of what employees need and use this intel to offer solutions that move your employees along on their financial wellness journey.

If you're worried that fintech is moving too fast . . . like a game of Double Dutch jump rope and you have no idea when to jump in, beware of that mentality. Don't sit on your hands for too long. Other employers are already making use of fintech and big data to evolve their offerings and make themselves more attractive to incoming generations of younger workers. While they may be at varying sophistication levels, you certainly don't want to find yourself stuck in an old model and mindset that puts you behind the pack of other employers competing for the same talent as you.

Employers who are lagging must catch up by leaning hard into technology now in order to solve employees' most challenging problems and to offer a "stickier" value proposition as an employer of choice.

Financial technology and data will help you better understand your employee base, where they are struggling, and what solutions are best for them. And, especially beneficial if you operate with a lean staff and tight budgets, harnessing what they both offer will make it possible to have a highly targeted, cost-efficient, internal segmentation strategy within your benefits lineup and reach your employees efficiently, with solutions that matter and in a way that respects their privacy.

Questions to consider

- Are we leveraging readily available data in order to understand our employee base and better target the benefits we're offering?

- Have we talked through the next five years and how we can use data and technology to target our benefits and lower costs while helping improve outcomes for employees?

- Do we have a plan for how we might be able to use tools like data and AI to make more strategic decisions about our benefits?

- Do we know where to start or are we avoiding the question because we don't know where to start?

- Are we leveraging our benefit and plan design consultants and vendors to make the highest and best use of any technology and data we may have access to today (e.g., such as for microtargeting of solutions to employee groups who need them)?

11

THE CONVERGENCE OF HEALTH CARE AND FINANCIAL CARE: TWO SIDES OF THE SAME COIN

"Take care of your body. It's the only place you have to live."

—Jim Rohn, American entrepreneur, author, and motivational speaker

There is an utterly undeniable link between our personal health and our wealth. More specifically, between the two major components of our individual health—the physical and the emotional—and our financial wellness, or our wealth. Pick your metaphor: legs of a stool, two sides of a coin, peanut butter and jelly. Whatever metaphor helps you get your mind around it can work. As I talk to employers and employees around the country, I also tend to think of them as essential gears in a machine: each part must be well oiled, clean, and working in harmony in the life of an employee in order for them to maintain wellness, manage their lives, and have the peace of mind and focus to be an effective contributing member of your team. If one area of their life isn't working optimally or develops even a minor problem, the machine might hobble along for a while . . . but it will eventually wear down, damage the other parts, or break down completely.

Innovation in science, health care, psychology, technology, behavioral economics, human capital, social media, employee benefits, and other domains of modern life have finally come together to bring into the workplace the recognition that employee health and financial wellness (and ultimately business performance) are inextricably related. Financial stress affects employee mental and physical health. Similarly, mental or physical health problems can have dire consequences for employees financially. Employees experiencing stress on *any* of these fronts can't possibly perform their best at work, which can, in turn, affect employee performance. As we've examined at many points in this book, these elements move in tandem—for better or worse.

As consumers, we caught on to this connection years ago. That's primarily because as individuals we experience these interconnections in our own lives.

But it's taken decades for employers to fully appreciate the interdependence between all the components of employee well-being and, in turn, the impact of the employee's well-being on the business. It has also taken changing demographics in the workforce, an entire generation of employees (namely

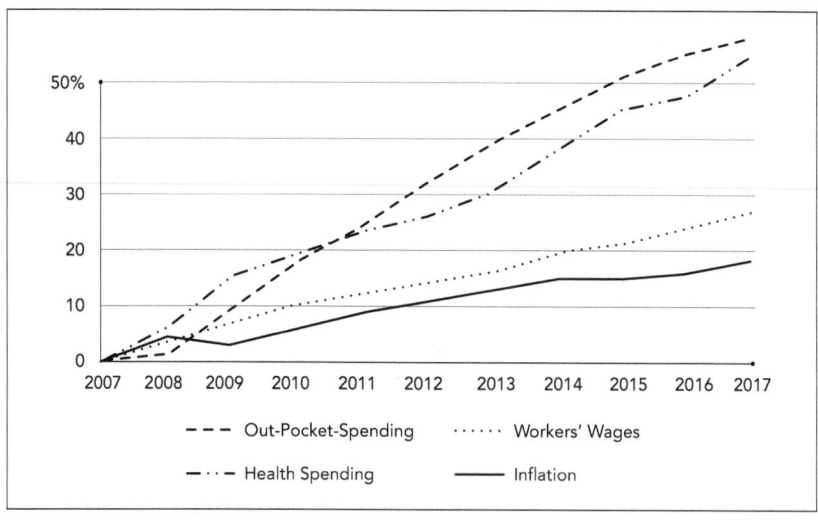

For years, out-of-pocket spending on health care has far outpaced inflation and workers' wages. This burden has plagued employees for years and will continue to do so in the absence of radical changes in marketplace dynamics. Employers and the combination of health and financial wellness benefits they provide are often the only protection workers have from this harsh reality.

Millennials) to come along and force this awareness front and center at work. As we examined in Chapter 6, these are employees who see little or no distinction between work life and personal life, who wear their hearts on their sleeves on social media and with employers, who are looking to employers to care for them in most areas of their lives. Add to this mix our complex personal lives that went on full display in Zoom meetings during COVID, a growing movement in conscious capitalism, and new levels of employer empathy, and we have a society that's now wide awake to the fact that employees can't function at their best if any part of their physical, emotional, or financial houses is out of order.

In the back of our minds, we have long known intuitively that there is a strong connection between finances and overall health. There is a reason that literally thousands of experts and authors, from Dave Ramsey to Pete the Planner to Suze Orman to Thomas Stanley, author of the seminal *The Millionaire Next Door* . . . have touched on the connection between money, health, and overall well-being and continued to beat the drum to anyone who would listen. The problem was, unfortunately, very few were listening, as there wasn't hard data supporting it, and there wasn't a willing and captive audience.

We have highlighted in previous chapters that before about 2016 or so, the idea of total employee wellness was not really a bona fide "thing" in corporate boardrooms or in water-cooler vernacular. But since that time, there's been a dawning realization that financial wellness and personal wellness go hand-in-hand. Then events like the 2020 COVID-19 pandemic simply brought it all out into the open, and the fragile connections were right there for us to see. COVID did tremendous financial, physical, and emotional damage to a lot of people. It has eviscerated entire industries, caused immense personal stress and separation, and triggered financial hardship and anxiety, the likes of which we've never before experienced.

But this is a book meant to have a shelf life, and COVID is just a moment in time. Why would I risk talking about it? Because it's a watershed event for society and for employers. For those who know me, I'm an optimist, a glass-half-full kind of person. I tend to look for the silver lining in everything, and I've done the same when it comes to the COVID calamity. I think it's pushed us from a mindset of, "Well, I know these things are related, but..." to a fully enlightened recognition of the interconnectivity and fragility of our financial, physical, and emotional well-being. It's highlighted the ever-growing role of the employer as the facilitator and provider of wellness solutions. And it's underscored the fact that that if we have a health crisis (mental or physical), it directly impacts our financial house and vice versa. It accelerated our thinking by six years in six months.

We have been hit over the head, essentially. We know once and for all we can't stick our head in the sand about how these components of well-being relate. As they say in the South, "That dog don't hunt."

Many employers, in order to keep their businesses and people together at the seams, have jumped in to provide whatever support they could. Some began offering tools to help employees build emergency savings like UPS did with the help of Voya, Blackrock, and others. Some made the incredibly hard decision to stop 401(k) matches in order to avoid furloughs and layoffs. Some turned on a dime to expand their mental health offerings. On the one hand, they were trying to conserve costs and preserve the business, while juggling the needs of their most important asset—their employees. Benefits, unlike compensation, show you care. They show your employees you actually have a heart. That you are, in fact, all in this together. Families and empathetic companies help one another. Not that money doesn't matter (especially for those struggling to make ends meet), but it reminded us, for instance, that without our health and sanity, little else matters. The priority of money for money's sake had lessened, if only momentarily and only in cases where we needed to focus on what really matters. I mean, really matters. And that's why having a complete safety net of benefits helps us keep the gears of our physical health, mental health, and financial health in some sort of working order all at the same time.

Almost overnight, we found ourselves in a new world. The walls came down between work and home. We see our employees' pets, their sick kids in diapers, their cramped home offices, their anxiety over catching COVID, their gyrating 401(k) investments, laid bare.

But what we have to realize, as employers, is that this isn't a fad. COVID was merely a catalyst for the last stage of change that was already coming. First, we can't unsee what we've seen, thanks to COVID. Second, we have evolved as a society and come to a place where the level of consciousness has been raised. It's been a long time coming. It's already been ten years since the Founder of Whole Foods, John Mackey, forced a paradigm shift with his book, *Conscious Capitalism.* In the years in between, companies have launched all manner of benefits programs designed to link health, fitness, emotional well-being, and money and financial incentives, from offering bonuses for completing health assessments to giving out the proverbial Fitbit. Fast-forward to the current day and leading organizations of executives, like the Business Roundtable mentioned in Chapter 7, have gone on record acknowledging that business must do more than engage in commerce; rather, it must be a good corporate citizen, and central to that is being compassionate and caring about the whole person that is the employee.

In short, the curtain that was slowly being drawn back before 2020 to reveal the connection between wealth and health was finally ripped open for us all to see the truth: health and wealth are inseparable, and the employer has willingly or unwillingly been crowned as a guardian of both.

We have a choice as employers: we can view this as a burden, one more worry for management and one more cost to add drag to the bottom line. Or, we can see it for the opportunity I believe it is: an opportunity for employers to visibly demonstrate compassion and provide meaningful solutions that will help employees get and keep their financial, physical, and emotional houses in order. We can try to deny or defend opinions to the contrary, but reality tells us this will benefit the employee, society, *and* business.

Employers who are not on this train better hop on at the next stop, because if you can't show you have a heart, an ounce of compassion, and an understanding of the hardships your employees have been experiencing, when the broader economy roars back—as it inevitably will—your Millennial workers will be walking out the door and across the street to another employer who shows they care by offering benefits that current and future employees want and need most.

This gives employers a prime opportunity to think more strategically and holistically about benefits spending and how to best deploy the money and resources you have that will give employees the greatest benefit in terms of their personal and financial wellness.

Quick history tour: early attempts to connect health and wealth

For the past fifteen years, the most obvious symbol of efforts to connect health and wealth has been the health savings account (HSA). As we covered in Chapter 4—on the burden of health-care expenses—the confluence between health and wealth is epitomized in HSAs, which were introduced in 2000. It was a major development in that it was one of the earliest emblems of the growing recognition by legislators and employers of the convergence between employee money and health. But while the market has slowly embraced this powerful tax-advantaged account, it hasn't held the magical answer to skyrocketing health-care costs or drastically improved our well-being. It has, however, as public policy goes, followed a reliable playbook for changing consumer-employee behavior, and that is a playbook we can continue to draw from. It's tax-advantaged—and, in this case, triple tax free (you never pay tax on this money as long as it's used for any kind of health-care expense) and is attached to payroll (making it easy and automatic for employees who choose to enroll). It followed the 401(k) playbook for a reason: we know that when we do things like make benefits tax deductible, automate them, and educate people effectively on how they work, we have a recipe for success. We now have to keep carrying those learnings forward and continue to find ways to improve employee health and wealth. Why? Because employees expect it, they need it, their well-being depends on it, and the well-being of our businesses depend on it.

Another watershed moment was when companies began to entice employees to make better health decision and encouraged them to focus on physical fitness. Demonstrably healthier employees translate into lower health-care costs in the market. So one small step for man, one giant leap for . . . employers.

We know the best place to start is with baby steps. It's like training for an Iron Man or marathon. It's all about one step at a time, just putting one foot in front of the other until you've gone 26.2 miles. When the Fitbit was introduced to corporate America in 2012, it was a watershed moment. It is a small piece of plastic that fits on your wrist and counts your daily steps, measures your heart rate, and provides some basic average health stats. Companies loved it. It was easy to understand and use, and represented a quantum leap in user interface and technology. They even had target of 10,000 daily steps, which is a nice round, but somewhat arbitrary number. But the optics of 10,000 was good, consumers found it palatable and doable, and the Fitbit started a movement that has had some decent staying power.

I also harken back to the original "standard" matching contributions in 401(k) plans of 50 percent up to 6 percent. Why are we matching to 6 percent? Who came up with that number? Who came up with the 50 percent up to 6 percent of pay? What does that mean? Shooting for a 6 percent savings rate sounds like a nice goal (in 1986 maybe), but it doesn't accomplish anything other than provide a beginning point in your savings plan. We should be saving 12–15 percent of our pay if we want to have any hope of being able to meet our most basic needs in retirement. But something about 6 percent sounds doable to many people and it's a step in the right direction. It was also heavily marketed by Fidelity in the 80s and 90s and became the de facto standard. As a matter of fact, if you ask a classroom of CFOs or HR directors like the ones who attend my class at the University of Chicago why we do this, they look back at me blankly and say something to the effect of "that's just what we've always done." The takeaway for employers here is to keep an eye out for those small "nudge" opportunities, those small ways we can help employees take another small step in the direction of financial wellness.

Friends of mine were also the first investors in what at the time was known as "Healthy Metrics Research." Yes, I like the name Fitbit better, too. The market did, too. (That's a minor point in this story but happens to be a great reminder that product and solution names matter in driving adoption among consumers.)

Time to break down silos and rethink priorities: from foosball to a holistic strategy

According to a 2019 Prudential report regarding health and wealth, ". . . employers who help their employees on both fronts stand the best chance of achieving the benefits that wellness programs can offer: healthier, happier, more productive employees whose physical and emotional health may lead to lower rates of absenteeism, fewer delayed retirements, and reduced levels of employee turnover, health-care costs, and employee disability."[1]

Heat map: Levels of discomfort during the patient healthcare journey

According to a national Experian Health study among 1,000 consumers, top "pain points" relate to finances

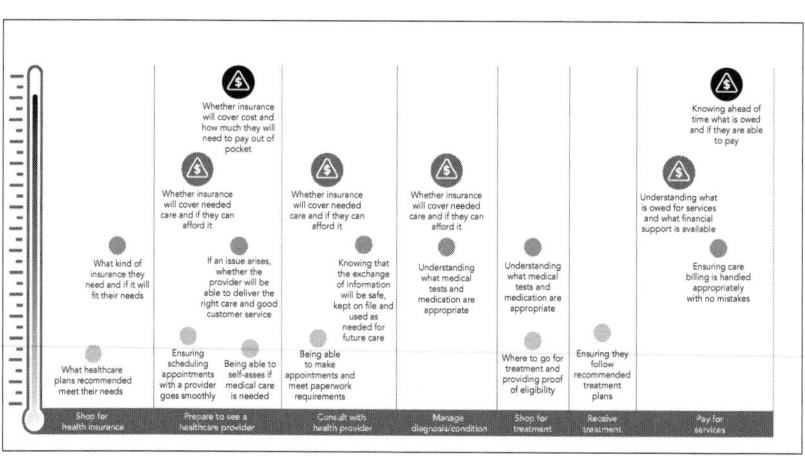

While many employers I talk with readily see the shift change that's occurred, it's worth calling out if you have any doubt. We now are more aware than ever of the critical but fragile links between physical, mental, and financial wellness. The decade-long obsession we had with cereal bars, happy hours, open floorplans (that benefited office furniture companies and drove employees insane), and mandatory "fun" is done. Oh, wait, I'm not finished making fun of employers yet: I have seen offices with tree houses, zip lines, mobile happy hour bars, in-house breakfast buffets filled with avocado toast and granola, froyo machines, pool tables, pong tournaments, axe throwing, entire wings for gamers, all introduced under the guise of helping their employees think more clearly, focus more efficiently, and be more loyal to the employer, to each other, and happier. A few short years ago, we were dazzled by all these things. Now, we're dazzled by things that make us feel more in control of our lives and sleep better at night.

But it didn't take long for us to all grow up a bit, and it's what we wanted, right? We've all been forced to turn our attention back to what really matters and to reallocate limited employee benefit resources accordingly. Any employer still in doubt about this should take a pause and ask why. But we now know that when push comes to shove, what's important is helping employees have better health, some semblance of peace of mind even during times of upheaval, and do whatever we can to stabilize them and give them a hand up so that they can keep taking steps forward that will advance them on their financial wellness journey. If we, as employers and advisors, are able to do that, we will directly be able to change their life trajectory and improve their financial and life outcomes.

How about that benefits strategic plan after all?

Just as other complex business or societal problems require an interdisciplinary, 360-degree approach, so does total employee wellness. Rather than thinking in silos and operating benefits in silos (the retirement plan committee in one part of the organization and the "rest" of the benefits committee in another part of the organization), we need to operate them in coordination to ensure we're thinking about the total person and the total impact of the benefits we're providing. Because at the end of the day, we can't afford to offer everything. But what we can do is act where there's the biggest need. If a house was on fire, you wouldn't be worried about which curtains to buy. If you had a Pacific Heights house with major cracks in the foundation, you wouldn't be installing a hot tub. We have to think the same way about benefits and take a disciplined approach to offering those benefits that are going to help employees tackle the biggest impediments to their physical, emotional, and ultimately their financial well-being.

This is a prescription we can use to deliver help where employees need it most.

**"Yes, we have an employee health plan.
Once a week we stuff donuts into the shredder."**

Using our knowledge for good

I won't bore you with rehashing the stats covered in previous chapters. But it's eye-opening to recap what we've covered and what we now know:

- We know that with increased financial stability comes increased health, lower health-care costs, and a longer life expectancy.

- We know that money and finances are one of the greatest stressors and sources of distraction and lost productivity among our employees.

- We know that, despite the wild proliferation of information available through the internet and other sources, financial literacy in this country is nowhere near what it could be.

- We know the relationship between the employer and employee has changed forever and that generations like Millennials expect their employer to help them with every aspect of their well-being, and they will be loyal to employers who deliver these benefits.

- We know that employees are struggling to manage virtually every aspect of their health-care costs, from premiums to deductibles to copays to prescription drugs.

- We have an absolute treasure trove of insight into human behavior thanks to the field of behavioral economics, and that tells us how to best understand and motivate people to take desired actions.

- We know that some of the biggest hurdles to employee financial wellness and peace of mind about money are student loan debt, lack of emergency savings, credit card debt, housing expenses, medical expenses, and retirement and post-retirement planning.

- We know that we have more data than ever on employees and consumers and that we have state-of-the-art analytics tools we can use to examine that data judiciously and ethically to gain insight into what's happening in virtually every aspect of a person's life (not to mention the ability we have to anticipate what might happen next!).

- We know that the technology and venture capitalists that have poured hundreds of billions of dollars into the health care, insurance, and fintech industries all recognize the gravity and scope of these problem and are constantly innovating and offering solutions that can appeal to employees and give them tools that can make a real difference in their lives.

If you look at each of these realities in isolation, they may not seem like much. But when you look at them in their totality, it's a pretty glorious view. We see that, as employers, we can be empowered to look at benefits and employee wellness in a new light. We can let ourselves off the hook from doing things the way we've always done them *starting today, starting now.*

By taking a pause, we can look at our employees and at our benefits in a much more strategic, holistic way and offer benefits that are going to drive the best possible outcomes for employees and for business. Let's take this knowledge and use it to make more strategic, thoughtful decisions about benefits and focus on a more prescriptive model that's going to provide benefits that address the greatest problems employees are facing. After all, if a patient had diabetes, a doctor wouldn't suggest an arm splint. If you found someone who had been wandering in the desert, you wouldn't offer them discounted tickets to a Counting Crows show or an amusement park. You'd offer them emergency medical care and water because that's what they need the most.

All this information we now have—about demographics, about the state of financial literacy in this country, about the incredible innovation in fintech, about the science that shows the connection between our physical, mental, and financial health—is an incredible treasure trove. It's a moment when we can take a pause, recognize what our employees are facing now and what we expect them to face in the future, and begin to offer a holistically designed, highly targeted suite of benefits that will have the greatest impact in their lives and in your business.

The call for employers: re-balance your efforts, then focus on execution at "the last mile"

You may feel like you already think holistically about employees, or this may be new territory for you. Or you may feel like your benefits budget is absolutely tapped out because of all the expanded benefits you so generously rolled out as a result of COVID. Or you may not care. You may think that if you offer a basic health plan and 401(k), that should be good enough.

The truth is, I have sat in hundreds of meetings where 1) there's a tendency to ignore the broader idea of financial wellness and focus only on the 401(k) plan, and 2) the health insurance plan dominates the whole conversation. I've also seen countless employers be penny wise and pound foolish when it comes to investing in benefits. I get it.

Wherever you are, it's critical to recognize the connection between health and financial wellness and to recognize what a powerful tool in hiring and retention you have when you find ways to address the two sides of the coin: financial well-being and physical well-being—both health and wealth for your employees. It's also important to recognize that if you take a step back and begin to have some candid conversations with your leadership team and with your benefits consultants, you just might discover that you can make even minor shifts in how you allocate your benefits dollars, and by doing so make an enormous impact in the lives of your employees. The part that employers often find most surprising is that for a minimal amount of money (especially relative to the cost of health plan premiums!), we can introduce new benefits that make a huge total impact for employees in both their health and finances simultaneously.

As an entrepreneur and employer, I understand the temptation to look at things only through the lens of the cost to the business. But society has evolved, and we have to evolve with it. And the best part is, we now have the knowledge and the technology and the marketplace of solutions at our disposal that can allow us to move the needle for employees and our business by thinking more holistically about the total health and financial wellness of our current and future employees. We know what employees want: solutions that are easy to use, convenient, automated yet personalized, engaging, and delivered in the manner and channel they choose (digital, mobile, video, in person, or a mix of them all). And we know there are countless solutions available that we can offer cost effectively while helping them address the biggest problems they face, from student loan debt to the struggle to build up emergency savings. All we have to do is step back and make some small shifts, and we can truly make an enormous impact for our employees and the businesses we are tasked with managing profitably.

Where does the retiree health care money go?

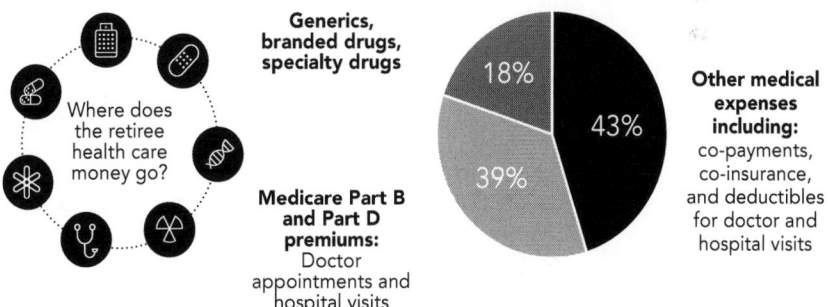

A typical couple aged 65 in 2020 was expected to need approximately $295,000 in after-tax dollars saved to cover health-care expenses in retirement, such as insurance costs, drugs and Medicare premiums. It's no wonder so many older employees are scared to make the leap into retirement.

Source: https://www.fidelity.com/viewpoints/personal-finance/plan-for-rising-health-care-costs

It's an opportunity to demonstrate to employees that you recognize they are human and more than a mere labor resource. Even if you can't drastically increase your benefits spending, I assure you that you can challenge yourself and your team to take a hard look at these trends, talk with your employees, and work with your benefits providers and retirement consultants. Take every possible step to ensure the benefits you and your employees are investing in are all pointed toward creating the greatest possible health and financial outcomes.

In the future, the employers who win in this game will be the ones who, like the best online retailers, figure out how to take all this knowledge and technology we have and put it into action most effectively in what's known in the supply chain world as "the last mile." It's going to be about how we get the internet to the house, how we get the package to the door. How we pick the right benefits from the right providers and deliver them to employees in a way that's truly engaging and useful in their lives. The employers who take the time to make moves in this direction will be the ones that in the future will stand out compared to other employers and deliver benefits their employees will be truly grateful for, for years to come. It's a combination of education and prioritizing, including some of these prescriptively into benefit packages and helping people change their behavior by rewarding the decisions we desire that produce the outcomes we want. If Fitbit helped millions of people get into the habit of walking, what might we be able to achieve next?

Questions to consider

- Did we realize fully how interconnected these topics are in the lives and minds of our employees?

- Do we have a true realization of how physical, mental, and financial health all affect each other?

- If we have separate groups managing our various wellness solutions, are they talking to each other and thinking holistically about our benefits?

PART IV
CONCLUSION

Bringing it all together: from an outdated model to a modern prescription for total financial wellness

In Chapter 3, we discussed the unmistakably vivid metaphor of the rock climber trying to safely overcome the overhang of credit card debt. That image comes to mind now, as we consider the challenge before us. It might look insurmountable, but with the right tools, careful thought, and deliverable movements, we can work past the seemingly insurmountable and complete the climb to financial wellness. We just have to think about our tools, our safety gear, our fellow climbers, and the reward we stand to gain from our efforts.

First, I want to thank you for joining me in this examination of financial wellness in the workplace and why it has become one of the top imperatives for employers. Second, I want to congratulate you. I believe if you're open to the ideas I've presented here, and have been willing to come this far in the book, you very likely have what it takes to act on the information I've provided, and to do it in a way that will help your existing and future employees contribute to society as a whole and make your business a better corporate citizen.

And you also are already climbing in the right direction to make your employees and your business more resilient in an increasingly fast-moving and uncertain world.

As I've repeated multiple times throughout the book, I'm not suggesting you become an expert in demographics, financial services, behavioral finance, technology, or any other discipline mentioned within. What matters is that, as employers, we open our eyes to the current reality, make ourselves aware of the big patterns affecting our employees and our business, and do the best we can to inform ourselves about what's ahead—as we think about doing what's smart relative to our existing employees, and think about what we need to be doing now and in the months and years ahead to attract and retain the next generation of our workforce.

We've looked at the biggest financial obstacles standing squarely between American workers and their financial wellness and peace of mind:

- Mountains of student loan debt that's eating up cash flow and preventing employees from making real progress in building emergency and retirement savings.

- Credit card debt that continues to pile up as more and more consumers fail to pay off balances and rely on credit cards to cover basic expenses.

- Health-care costs, which continue to skyrocket for the healthy and sick, young and old, alike.

- Housing costs, which continue to consume significant amounts of workers' monthly income.

Then we looked at key trends that employers of all sizes should be keeping an eye on and factoring into their benefits strategy (and more importantly, into their financial wellness strategy):

- Demographics that show us what current and incoming workers look like and what they want and need—especially Millennials, which form the largest, most influential, and most demanding core of the workforce—and the need to appreciate the texture of the diversity, equity, and inclusion mosaic.

- The changing nature of the employer-employee relationship, which has made the employer the parent and provider-in-chief of wellness solutions to employees at virtually every phase and milestone of their adult working lives.

- The behavioral economics that tell us virtually everything we need to know about humans and how we behave when it comes to money, and how specifically we can nudge individuals to make better short- and long-term financial decisions.

- Consumerism, which shapes how we shop for everything, including workplace benefits, and how we want products and services delivered to us in every part of our lives.

- The convergence of financial, mental, and physical wellness and why we, as employers, can no longer afford to look at them as separate and distinct realms.

- The trends in tech and big data that give us an unprecedented ability to understand employees and offer them state-of-the-art benefits.

If we plot a basic prescription for success visually, it's quite simple, actually.

At the end of the day, the goal is to get you to step back, think about your employee benefits in a more modern and holistic way, and recognize the fact that we have the unique ability to change the course of the health, wealth, and life outcomes of our employees. We can make a difference in whether they succeed in their journey upward, or whether they are left struggling or even in danger.

A prescriptive approach can help employees get and keep their financial house in order

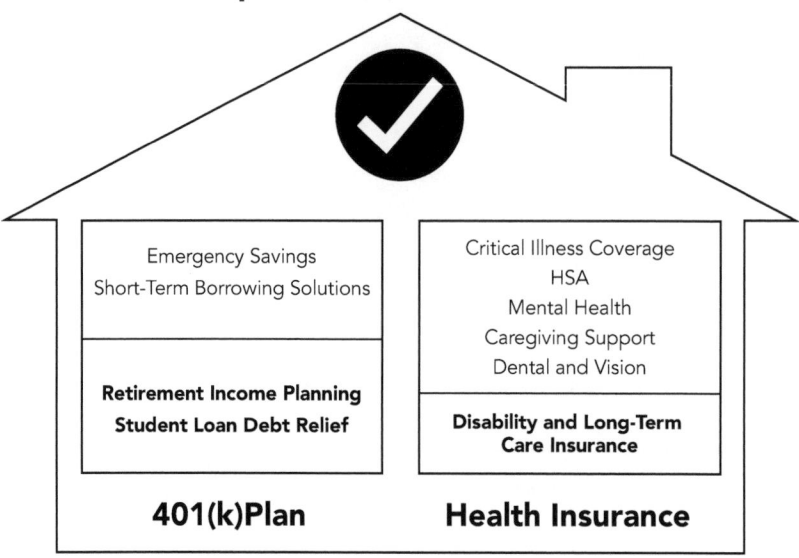

These essential solutions should be at the heart of virtually every employee benefits strategy. They work together to protect and advance the financial wellness of all generations of adult employees.

We've talked through the biggest impediments your employees face in trying to achieve any modicum of financial wellness. While I can't help you completely future-proof your business, I can use what I've learned to help you and your team be more prepared to take steps now toward making sure you're offering benefits that are moving the needle in the areas that we now know matter the most to your employees and will make the greatest impact on their lives and create the greatest value and stickiness between you and the workforce of the future. I have a deep understanding and appreciation of the ethos of the American employee and also understand the enormous capacity we as employers have in making a difference in the lives of our employees.

And know I'm not asking you to chase a shiny rock or run from one side of the boat to the other. No business can afford to do that for very long. These struggles and needs that employees have and their expectations of you as their employer are not fly-by-night fads—these are clear, persistent signals that have been growing stronger and stronger by the year and should be factored into the benefits and hiring retention plans of any business that wants to be responsive, resilient, competitive, and deliver on the promises you make to employees.

Small changes can have a huge, positive impact for your employees and your business

The great news is that you don't have to upend your business in order to act on the information in this book. Just as you might with any other aspect of your business strategy, my suggestion is to step back and look for the low-hanging fruit—the areas where you can make small changes for the biggest impact.

You can look at making phased changes that sit at the intersection of:

- Minimal cost
- Ease of launch/implementation
- Ease of administration
- Employee need and impact

What's next?

While every company is different and the exact steps you take will be unique to you, there are a few immediate things you can do:

Get the left hand talking to the right hand. It's amazing to me how many companies don't have their benefits consultants talking to each other and cross-pollinating to share data and ideas. If you don't do this already, get your retirement plan folks and your health plan folks talking to each other about this bigger idea of financial wellness that requires both of their core competencies. They know your business, should have a great sense of employee needs, can help you benchmark, and can help you come up with new ideas you may not have considered on your own. In that same vein, have your benefits committee and your retirement or investment committee strategize together.

Look at the data you have and the data you need in order to make more informed next steps. You are most definitely sitting on a wealth of data. Look at your employee census and what you know. Look at what data your benefits partners and health insurance carriers have. What about the retirement plan record keeper? What does the information tell you that you can act on today? What gaps do you have and how can you fill them?

Get input from employees. This doesn't mean employees get to dictate your benefits lineup. But whether it's using surveys, focus groups, or some other mechanism, ask them what they need to achieve their own idea of financial wellness. This can go a long way to offering benefits they'll actually use and thank you for offering. You ask your customers what they need; you should also be asking employees what they need. Be aware that your employees don't know what they don't know. They rarely know what's available to them. And unless they are Millennials, they are averse to discussing their financial or wellness situation at all, even in survey form.

Recognize that financial education alone isn't enough. It has to be supported with real solutions that preferably take into account the principals of behavioral economics and are designed in a way that will prompt action and good habits. All education needs to be supported with an ecosystem of coaching, direction, technology, and an amount of incentives or gamesmanship to encourage people to act.

If you don't have a real financial wellness strategy for your employees, create one. If you have one, make sure it's up to date. What does financial wellness mean to you and your employees? Is it helping your employees achieve peace of mind? Is it helping them retire on time or when they so choose? Is it helping them develop a budget and plan for emergency savings? Is it helping them pay off their student loans? It needs to be strategic and inclusive, addressing the debt obstacles challenging your employees and a savings strategy that often eludes them, both of which causes deep long-term anxiety.

Create a road map for action. What can you start, stop, or continue? Think about changes you can make now, in three months, and at open enrollment.

Be ready for what's next

It should be clear at this point (if you haven't already experienced it firsthand) that employers are under more pressure than ever to deliver meaningful, relevant benefits that help employees tackle the most pressing needs they and their families have. That's regardless of your size or industry, whether you sit under the spotlight of the public market or are privately held. As I have repeated throughout this book, many of your competitors have already figured this out or are on their way to doing so.

I understand it may seem like a lot of pressure, a tall ask. But it's absolutely doable. We've reached a perfect moment in time where there is a huge need that we actually have the ability to fill for our fellow humans. Maybe it sounds a bit squishy, but we have a chance to make some history by choosing to place financial wellness front and center in our business strategy. We are arriving at a point where we will be able to deliver the right benefits to the right employee at just the right moment in their lives. And we have the data and tools to get started today. We just have to open our eyes to the business case for change and say "yes."

By taking heed and following this guidance, you can truly put yourself in a position to make a real difference for all your employees across every demographic. This can have countless benefits for your business and your employees.

For employees:

- Helps stabilize their financial situation

- Improves their mental health and peace of mind, which ultimately can improve physical health

- Enables them to build better financial behaviors and resiliency

- Helps them prepare to retire with confidence and dignity and with a true sense of well-being

- Proves that you care about them as more than just an employee or a commodity

- Gives them knowledge they can use literally for a lifetime

For your business:

- Enables your ability to deliver on your employer brand promise

- Makes good on your diversity, inclusion, and CSR promises by advancing the financial wellness of the most vulnerable segments of your employee base while also advancing the greater good

- Ensures you can meet the demands of the largest segment of the working population

- Advances a mindset that can help your business think more holistically and be more prepared and resilient, regardless of what temporary trends or shifts or external events may be happening

- Increases your total benefits ROI while potentially lowering your costs of hiring, retention, and turnover

- Prepares your older workers to "fly the nest"—retire on time and make way for the next generation

- Creates a real competitive advantage and differentiates you as an employer of choice

As I stated previously, I am an eternal optimist. And I believe that in business we can do well by doing good by our employees and society as a whole. As employers, we have an epic opportunity and a solemn responsibility to help our employees improve their financial wellness.

When we do this, everyone wins by moving together toward greater financial wellness.

So let's collectively gear up and embrace the challenges facing our businesses and employees, and help our employees climb from a place of financial stress to new heights of financial wellness.

Questions to consider

- Do we have room to refine or expand our definition of financial wellness?

- If we don't have a financial wellness strategy, what steps are we taking to create one?

- Are we offering solutions specifically targeted at helping move employees further along in their financial wellness journey?

- Which single executive is responsible for championing and spearheading financial wellness initiatives and where does that accountability reside?

- Where in our company are conversations about financial wellness taking place (i.e., which teams, functions)?

- Do we make financial wellness education a part of employee onboarding and a year-round topic, or do we only bring it up during open enrollment season?

- Are we really looking at employee financial wellness from a 360-degree view so that we truly understand and can genuinely empathize with all the financial pressures they face?

- Are we offering a mix of benefits that are helping employees solve their entire financial picture?

- Are we measuring the right things if we want to make a real difference for our employees and our business in terms of financial wellness outcomes? Do we need to revisit our KPIs?

- Are we offering any sort of total financial wellness, budgeting, or planning tools or technology so that employees can better manage their complete financial picture?

APPENDIX

Recommended Reading

Want to learn more about behavioral economics, the Millennial mindset, how we form habits, resiliency, and more? Here are some favorite books from my personal library. It includes titles I often recommend to my colleagues, friends, and students.

Author	Title
Dan Ariely	*Payoff: The Hidden Logic that Shapes our Motivations* *Predictably Irrational: The Hidden Forces that Shape our Decisions*
Shlomo Benartzi	*Save More Tomorrow: Practical Behavioral Finance Solutions to Improve 401(k) Plans*
James C. Collins	*Good to Great: Why Some Companies Make the Leap and Others Don't*

Chris Crowley	*Younger Next Year: Live Strong, Fit, and Sexy — Until You're 80 and Beyond*
Charles Duhigg	*The Power of Habit: Why We Do What We Do in Life and Business*
Malcolm Gladwell	*Outliers: The Story of Success* *Tipping Point*
Adam Grant	*Think Again: The Power of Knowing What You Don't Know*
Daniel Kahnemann	*Thinking Fast and Slow*
Dean Karlan, Jacob Appel	*More Than Good Intentions: Improving the Ways the World's Poor Borrow, Save, Farm, Learn, and Stay Healthy*
Art Laffer	*The End of Prosperity: How Higher Taxes Will Doom the Economy—If We Let It Happen*
Michael Lewis	*Liar's Poker* *Moneyball: The Art of Winning an Unfair Game* *The New New Thing: A Silicon Valey Story* *The Undoing Project: A Friendship that Changed our Minds*
Erin Lowry	*BROKE Millennial Series: Stop Living Paycheck to Paycheck and Get Your Financial Life Together (#GYFLT)!*
John Mackey and Rajendra Sisodia	*Conscious Capitalism: Liberating the Heroic Spirit of Business*

Robin Sharma	*The Leader Who Had No Title: A Modern Fable on Real Success in Business and in Life* *The Monk Who Sold his Ferrari: A Fable About Fulfilling Your Dreams and Reaching Your Destiny*
Jay Shetty	*Think Like a Monk: Train Your Mind for Peace and Purpose Every Day*
Robert Shiller George Akerlof	*Narrative Economics: How Stories Go Viral and Drive Major Economic Events* *Animal Spirits: How Human Psychology Drives the Economy, and Why It Matters for Global Capitalism*
Nassim Nicholas Taleb	*The Black Swan: The Impact of the Highly Improbable*
Richard Thaler	*Nudge: Improving Decisions About Health, Wealth and Happiness* *Misbehaving: The Making of Behavioral Economics*
Charles Wheelan, Burton G. Malkiel	*Naked Money: A Revealing Look at our Financial System* *Naked Statistics: Stripping the Dread from the Data* *Naked Economics: Undressing the Dismal Science*

Questions to Consider:

Chapter 1—Financial Wellness

- How are we defining financial wellness? Are we thinking as broadly as we could be about financial wellness?

- Do we have an actual strategy for financial wellness, or do we have a collection of employee benefits?

- For companies that may be competing for our talent, how are they approaching financial wellness? Why are we doing what we do?

- Relative to the financial wellness of our employees, what are the ideal outcomes for our business? For our employees?

- How do our financial wellness-related benefits support our diversity and inclusion strategy?

- Do we understand that 75 percent of our employee base is living with some sort of financial anxiety every day?

- Do we recognize that while the anxieties are the same, the solutions for different cohorts are different? One size does not fit all, which may be the case with many of our existing benefits.

- How are we showing our employees that we care about them as human beings, and how is that reflected in our financial and well-being strategy?

- Have we ever attempted to measure the impact that our employees' financial stress is having on our business? In terms of lost productivity, forexample?

Chapter 2—Student Loan Debt

- What percentage of our employees are Millennials?

- Given that the number of employers offering some sort of student loan debt relief has doubled each year for the past five years, have we discussed this possibility in a meaningful way?

- What percentage of our employees have student loan debt?

- Have we evaluated specific student loan debt solutions for our employees?

- Do we realize just how easy payroll deduction programs are to implement?

- Do we know what our competitors are doing to help employees manage student loan debt?

- Have our employees expressed interest or need in getting some form of help managing their student loan debt?

- Do we understand just how much more our employees could be saving for retirement if they could knock out any student loan debt?

- Are we aware of the Abbot case study and have we discussed how it might apply to our business?

- Is our management team fully aware that Millennials consider student loan debt relief to be the most important workplace benefit?

- Do we know the approximate total amount of student loan debt our employees are carrying?

- Are members of our management team resistant to offering student loan debt solutions to employees? If so, why?

Chapter 3—Credit Card Overhang

- Without doing any research, do I know offhand the exact interest rates on each of my credit cards? Can our employees answer this question about their own credit cards?

- Beyond the provision to borrow from their retirement savings, have we evaluated or are we offering other lending solutions that might help employees minimize or at least better manage their credit card usage when they have tight cash flow (e.g., emergency/cash savings tools, payroll advances at fair rates, etc.)?

- Do we offer any options through a credit union, such as cash savings, payroll advances, or something other than credit cards?

- Are we offering any education on the perils of accumulating credit card debt?

- What can we do to change our employees' behavior and the relationship they have with their credit cards?

Chapter 4—Medical Debt

- Do our managers and employees know that extraordinary medical expenses are the leading cause of bankruptcy in the U.S.?

- Are we offering the right mix of voluntary benefits that provide employees with the best possible safety net for managing health-care expenses not covered by our health plan?

- Are we showcasing our voluntary health/medical and disability benefits in a way that employees can easily understand them and how they complement each other?

- For any employee, including executives, do we truly understand our disability coverage and exactly what it provides?

- If we have low uptake on voluntary benefits such as critical illness or hospital indemnity, do we know why employees are not enrolling?

- How are we prioritizing our total benefits spend between health and financial wellness and are we considering them together as part of a holistic strategy?

Chapter 5—Housing Expenses

- Are we fully aware of housing costs in the areas where our employees work and live, as well as the total impact of those costs on their financial wellness?

- Do we have any credit union, mortgage comparison tools, or other vendors or partners that can help employees better understand and manage housing costs?

- Are we offering employees basic tools and education to help employees assess and manage their housing-related costs more effectively?

Chapter 6—Shifting Demographics

- Do we have a detailed understanding of the demographics of our employee base?

- What percentage of our employees will or should ideally be retiring in next five years?

- Do we have a plan in place to help Boomers generate and manage retirement income?

- What is our strategy for employees nearing retirement (e.g., buyout strategy or other)?

- Do we have a strategy and specific, relevant solution for each of the segments of our employee population? Solutions for each cohort—a strategy and a plan for each segment of our population?

- Do we have a solid handle on our current census and demographics?

- How have our employee demographics changed and have we planned specifically for how they might change in the future?

- How are we interacting with each demographic segment when it comes to wellness? Do we understand important differences not only across age groups, but across racial and ethnic segments of our employee base?

- How are we educating our employees on budgeting, planning, debt management, emergency savings, digital advice, financial wellness apps, and retirement income planning?

Chapter 7—The Changing Relationship Between Employer and Employee

- How has our company's role in the lives of our employees changed or expanded?

- Are we as prepared as we need to be to understand what financial wellness benefits our employee are going to want and expect from us, and are we prepared to respond quickly?

- What training are we offering to our benefits teams to help them anticipate the financial wellness needs of our employees? Are we offering our benefits team the data to help them anticipate trends and needs?

- How has our relationships with our employees changed, and how do we see it changing in the future?

- Have we reflected on how it's changed over the years?

- Are we prepared for the 100 million Millennials who are only now integrating into the workforce?

Chapter 8—The Undeniable Force of Behavioral Economics

- Did we realize just how much influence behavioral economists have had on how workplace benefits are designed (e.g., automatic payroll deduction, company matching, program rewards and incentives)?

- What can we learn from this academic research?

- How can we help nudge our employee base to make better financial decisions? How can we better help them help themselves?

- Are we integrating gamification, rewards, and encouragement to drive better uptake of certain benefits?

- In what ways are we seeing some of the principles of behavioral economics playing out in how our employees choose and use the benefits we offer?

- How are we keeping a pulse on the latest developments in behavioral economics?

- Have we ever discussed this as a team, or have we ever considered doing something like a book club that looks at some of the many books written by leading social scientists, organizational behaviorists, and behavioral economists?

Chapter 9—The Growth of Consumerism

- Are we treating employees like consumers or clients with particular needs and preferences?

- Do our current offerings, as well as our rollouts, delivery, and ongoing support, reflect the same seamless, frictionless convenience our employees experience when purchasing goods and services in the "outside" world?

- Are we meeting the demands of our employees in terms of how they want to interact with our business and the benefits we offer?

- Do we have an intranet where these consumers can evaluate options and make decisions on their benefits, retirement, investments, HSA, financial wellness?

Chapter 10—The Rise of Technology and Big Data: What It Means for Financial Wellness

- Are we leveraging readily available data in order to understand our employee base and better target the benefits we're offering?

- Have we talked through the next five years and how we can use data and technology to target our benefits and lower costs while helping improve outcomes for employees?

- Do we have a plan for how we might be able to use tools like data and AI to make more strategic decisions about our benefits?

- Do we know where to start or are we avoiding the question because we don't know where to start?

- Are we leveraging our benefit and plan design consultants and vendors to make the highest and best use of any technology and data we may have access to today (e.g., such as for microtargeting of solutions to employee groups who need them)?

Chapter 11—The Convergence of Health Care and Financial Care

- Did we realize fully how interconnected these topics are in the lives and minds of our employees?

- Do we have a true realization of how physical, mental, and financial health all affect each other?

- If we have separate groups managing our various wellness solutions, are they talking to each other and thinking holistically about our benefits?

NOTES

Introduction

De Guzman, Dianne. "Extreme Things College Graduates Would Do to Get Rid of Student Debt." *Connecticut Post.* February 17, 2016. https://www.ctpost.com/education/article/student-loan-debt-game-pinky-mike-tyson-6837420.php?forceWeb=1

Chapter 1 Epperson, Sharon, and Manning, Patrick. "Teaching Financial Education in Schools Finally Catches On." CNBC. February 5, 2020. https://www.cnbc.com/2020/02/04/teaching-financial-education-in-schools-finally-catches-on.html

[2] Consumer Financial Protection Bureau. "Financial Wellness at Work." nd. https://www.consumerfinance.gov/data-research/research-reports/financial-wellness-at-work/

[3] Davidson, Liz. "Considering a Financial Wellness Program for Your Employees: Make Sure You Ask These Questions First." *Forbes.* March 3, 2019. https://www.forbes.com/sites/financialfinesse/2019/03/03/considering-a-financial-wellness-program-for-your-employees-make-sure-you-ask-these-questions-first/#453814f62f3b

Chapter 2

Daniels, Mitch. "Mitch Daniels Op-Ed: A Fix for Student Loan Debt." *Chicago Tribune.* August 21, 2015. https://www.chicagotribune.com/opinion/commentary/ct-student-loan-debt-mitch-daniels-purdue-20150821-story.html

[2] Friedman, Zach. "Student Loan Debt Statistics in 2020: A Record $1.6 Trillion." *Forbes.* February 3, 2020. https://www.forbes.com/sites/zackfriedman/2020/02/03/student-loan-debt-statistics/?sh=4312a60d281f

[3] Maldonado, Camilo. "Price of College Increasing Almost 8 Times Faster Than Wages." *Forbes*. February 24, 2018. https://www.forbes.com/sites/camilomaldonado/2018/07/24/price-of-college-increasing-almost-8-times-faster-than-wages/?sh=5cacebf866c1

[4] Rathmanner, David. "February 2016 Student Loan Borrower Survey." Lendedu. February 8, 2016. https://lendedu.com/blog/february-student-loan-survey

[5] Abbott. "Got Student Debt? We Got You." June 26, 2019. https://www.abbott.com/corpnewsroom/strategy-and-strength/company-student-loan-perk.html

[6] Anderson, Brian. "SECURE Act Allows 529 Plans to Repay (Some) Student Loan Debt." *401K Specialist*. January 20, 2020. https://401kspecialistmag.com/secure-act-allows-529-plans-to-repay-some-student-loan-debt/

[7] Kagan, Julia. "Pension Protection Act of 2006." Investopedia. November 27, 2020. https://www.investopedia.com/terms/p/pensionprotectionact2006.asp#:~:text=The%20Pension%20Protection%20Act%20sought,their%20401(k)%20plan

[8] Aon Hewitt via PeanutButter. https://www.getpeanutbutter.com/industries-education/

[9] Hoffower, Hillary. "Millennials and Gen X Are Both Stressed, Broke, and in Debt—But Gen X Is More Worried About It." *Business Insider*. October 10, 2019. https://www.businessinsider.com/personal-finance/millennials-gen-x-money-stresses-retirement-savings-2019-10

[10] Young Workers and Student Debt Survey Report Methodology (February 2017), American Student Assistance. Available at file.asa.org.

[11] Abbott. "Got Student Debt?"

[12] Johnson Hess, Abigail. "Tuition at Public Colleges Has Increased in all 50 States Over the Past 10 Years—Here's How Your State Compares." CNBC. October 24, 2019. https://www.cnbc.com/2019/10/24/college-costs-have-

increased-in-all-50-states-over-the-past-10-years.html

[13] Financial Advisor. "The College Quandary Today." December 18, 2020. https://www.fa-mag.com/news/the-college-quandary-today-57554.html?section=47&page=3

Chapter 3

[1] Desjardins, Jeff. "Infographic: The 5,000-Year History of Consumer Credit." *Business Insider.* August 30, 2017. https://www.businessinsider.com/5000-year-history-of-consumer-credit-2017-8

[2] Amadeo, Kimberly. "Current U.S. Consumer Debt." *The Balance*, March 6, 2021. https://www.thebalance.com/consumer-debt-statistics-causes-and-impact-3305704

[3] Debt.org. "Key Figures Behind America's Consumer Debt." January 28, 2021. https://www.debt.org/faqs/americans-in-debt/#:~:text=Credit%2Dcard%20use%20took%20a,increased%20regulations%20over%20credit%20cards.

[4] Picchi, Aimee. "Here's a Top Reason Americans Are Carrying an Average Credit Card Balance of Over $6,200." *USA Today*. February 12, 2020 https://www.usatoday.com/story/money/2020/02/12/credit-card-debt-average-balance-hits-6-200-and-limit-31-000/4722897002/

[5] Lexington Law. "2020 Average Credit Card Debt Statistics in the U.S." January 4, 2020. https://www.lexingtonlaw.com/blog/credit-cards/average-credit-card-debt-statistics.html

[6] Pichee, Aimee. "Here's a Top Reason."

[7] Foster, Kevin; Green, Claire; and Stevins, Joanna. "The 2018 Survey of Consumer Payment Choice: Summary Results." Federal Reserve Bank of Atlanta. 2019. https://www.frbatlanta.org/-/media/documents/banking/consumer-payments/survey-of-consumer-payment-choice/2018/2018-survey-of-consumer-payment-choice.pdf

[8] Peter, Bianca. "Historical Credit Card Interest Rates." WalletHub. October 12, 2020. https://wallethub.com/edu/cc/historical-credit-card-interest-rates/25577/

[9] Shepherd, Maddie. "Cash vs. Credit Card Spending Statistics. (2021). Fundera https://www.fundera.com/resources/cash-vs-credit-card-spending-statistics

[10] Amadeo, Kimberly. "Average U.S. Credit Card Debt Statistics." The Balance. November 30, 2020. https://www.thebalance.com/average-credit-card-debt-u-s-statistics-3305919

[11] Lembo Stolba, Stefan. "Experian 2020 Consumer Credit Review." Experian. January 4, 2021. https://www.experian.com/blogs/ask-experian/consumer-credit-review/

[12] Pichee, Aimee. "Here's a Top Reason."

[13] Palmer, Kimberly. "How Gen X Can Start Tackling Its Credit Card Debt." NerdWallet. July 21, 2020. https://www.nerdwallet.com/article/credit-cards/pay-off-gen-x-credit-card-burden

[14] Horch, A. J. "Almost Half of America Is Now Carrying Credit Card Debt, and More of It." CNBC. May 4, 2020. https://www.cnbc.com/2020/05/04/almost-half-of-america-now-carrying-credit-card-debt-and-more-of-it.html

[15] Hoffower, Hillary. "Millennials and Gen X Are Both Stressed."

Chapter 4

[1] Santhanam, Laura. "Millennials Rack Up the Most Medical Debt, and More Frequently." PBS NewsHour. July 26, 2018. https://www.pbs.org/newshour/health/millennials-rack-up-the-most-medical-debt-and-more-frequently

[2] National Academy of Sciences. "Origins and Evolution of Employment-Based Health Benefits." 1993. https://www.ncbi.nlm.nih.gov/books/NBK235989/

[3] Konish, Lorie. "137 Million American Are Drowning in Medical Debt. Here's What to Know If You Need Some Relief." CNBC. November 12, 2019. https://www.cnbc.com/2019/11/10/americans-are-drowning-in-medical-debt-what-to-know-if-you-need-help.html

[4] Petrov, Christo. "25+ Medical Bankruptcy Statistics to Know in 2020." SpendMeNot. January 29, 2021. https://spendmenot.com/blog/medical-bankruptcy-statistics/

[5] Leonhardt, Megan. "32% of American Workers Have Medical Debt—and Over Half Have Defaulted on It." CNBC. February 13, 2020. https://www.cnbc.com/2020/02/13/one-third-of-american-workers-have-medical-debt-and-most-default.html

[6] Andrews, Michelle. "Why a Long-Term Disability Policy Is More Important than Pet Insurance." NPR. October 11, 2017. https://www.npr.org/sections/health-shots/2017/10/11/556946744/why-a-long-term-disability-policy-is-more-important-than-pet-insurance

[7] "Patients May be the New Payers, But Two in Three Do Not Pay Their Hospital Bills in Full." TransUnion. June 26, 2017. https://newsroom.transunion.com/patients-may-be-the-new-payers-but-two-in-three-do-not-pay-their-hospital-bills-in-full/

[8] Pyles, Sean. "Why So Many Millennials Are Plagued by Medical Debt and Why They Can Do. MarketWatch. January 9, 2019. https://www.marketwatch.com/story/why-so-many-millennials-are-plagued-by-medical-debt-and-what-they-can-do-2019-01-09#:~:text=It%20found%20that%20the%20frequency,at%20age%2027%2C%20at%20%24684

[9] O'Kane, Caitlin. "Elderly Couple Found Dead in Apparent Murder-Suicide, Left Notes About High Medical Bills." CBS News. August 9, 2019. https://www.cbsnews.com/news/elderly-couple-found-dead-in-apparent-murder-suicide-left-notes-about-high-medical-bills/

Chapter 5

Holeman, Nick. "Is Buying a Home a Good Investment?" Betterment. November 6, 2019. https://www.betterment.com/resources/buying-home-good-investment/

[2] Joint Center for Housing Studies of Harvard University. "America's Rental Housing 2020." 2020. https://www.jchs.harvard.edu/sites/default/files/Harvard_JCHS_Americas_Rental_Housing_2020.pdf

[3] S&P Dow Jones Indices. "S&P CoreLogic Case-Shiller U.S. National Home Price NSA Index." February 23, 2021. https://www.spglobal.com/spdji/en/indices/indicators/sp-corelogic-case-shiller-us-national-home-price-nsa-index/

[4] Leonhardt, Megan. "Millennials May Be Facing Unaffordable Housing, But They're Paying Less in Rent than Other Generations." CNBC. September 26, 2019. https://www.cnbc.com/2019/09/26/buying-a-house-is-pricier-for-millennials-but-renting-is-cheaper.html

[5] Leonhardt, Megan. "Millennials May Be Facing Unaffordable Housing."

[6] Hoffower, Hillary. "Student Loan Debt and Skyrocketing Housing Prices Have Become so Bad that More Millennials Are Planning to Rent Forever." *Business Insider*. November 20, 2019. https://www.businessinsider.com/more-millennials-planning-to-rent-forever-cant-afford-housing-2019-11

[7] Hoffower, Hillary. "Student Loan Debt and Skyrocketing Housing Prices."

[8] Van Der Meulen, Dan. "The Average Down Payment on a House Is Much Smaller Than You Think." HousingWire. July 1, 2019. https://www.housingwire.com/articles/49443-the-average-down-payment-is-much-smaller-than-you-think/

[9] MetLife. "4 Ways Your Employer Can Help You Buy a New Home." January 13, 2021. https://www.metlife.com/blog/insurance/employee-benefits-buying-a-home/

[10] National Housing Conference. "Employer-Assisted Housing: The Basics." nd. https://nhc.org/policy-guide/employer-assisted-housing-the-basics/#:~:text=Examples%20of%20employer%2Dassisted%20housing,attract%20and%20retain%20necessary%20employees.

Chapter 6

Kelly, Jack. "Nearly 30 Million Baby Boomers Forced into Unwanted Retirement." *Forbes*. November 19, 2020. https://www.forbes.com/sites/jackkelly/2020/11/19/nearly-30-million-baby-boomers-forced-into-unwanted-retirement/?sh=2d9016be5d7d

[2] Neal, Stephanie. "Are Companies About to Have a Gen X Retention Problem?" *Harvard Business Review*. July 26, 2019. https://hbr.org/2019/07/are-companies-about-to-have-a-gen-x-retention-problem

[3] Miller, Stephen. "Targeted Benefits Help Baby Boomers Stay at Work, Prepare to Retire." Society for Human Resource Management (SHRM). November 4, 2019. https://www.shrm.org/resourcesandtools/hr-topics/benefits/pages/targeted-benefits-help-baby-boomers-stay-at-work-prepare-to-retire.aspx

[4] Sardon, Maitane. "Millennials Prefer Apps to Humans, for Financial Advice." *The Wall Street Journal*. March 16, 2020. https://www.wsj.com/articles/millennials-prefer-apps-to-humans-for-financial-advice-11584377127?mod=searchresults_pos2&page=1

[5] O'Malley, Lisa. "The Millennial Job Hopping Myth." Bonfyreapp.com. nd. https://bonfyreapp.com/blog/the-millennial-job-hopping-myth

[6] Kelly, Jack. "Nearly 30 Million Baby Boomers Forced Into Unwanted Retirement." *Forbes*. November 19, 2020. https://www.forbes.com/sites/jackkelly/2020/11/19/nearly-30-million-baby-boomers-forced-into-unwanted-retirement/?sh=475bdc2a5d7d

7 Backman, Maurie. "Baby Boomers Are Worried About Healthcare Costs—So Why Aren't More Doing Something About It?" The Motley Fool. December 17, 2019. https://www.fool.com/retirement/2019/12/17/baby-boomers-are-worried-about-healthcare-costs-so.aspx

8 Jaworski, Barbara. "Top Ten Baby Boomer Myths that Will Hurt the Bottom Line." Monster. nd. https://hiring.monster.ca/employer-resources/recruiting-strategies/acquiring-job-candidates/baby-boomer-myths-that-will-hurt-the-bottom-line/

9 Neal, Stephanie. "Are Companies About to Have a Gen X Retention Problem?"

10 Napach, Bernice. "Gen Xers Are Falling Behind Financially." Benefits Pro. July 3, 2019. https://www.benefitspro.com/2019/07/03/gen-xers-are-falling-behind-financially-ebri-412-84340/

11 John Hancock Retirement Plan Services. "Gen X Needs Help with Financial Wellness While Planning for Retirement." October 2, 2019. https://retirement.johnhancock.com/us/en/viewpoints/financial-wellness/gen-x-needs-help-with-financial-wellness-on-the-way-to-retirement

12 Copeland, Craig. "Comparing the Financial Status of Gen X Families." Employee Benefit Research Institute (EBRI). June 27, 2019. https://www.ebri.org/content/summary/comparing-the-financial-status-of-generation-x-families

13 Moran, Gwen. "This Is What Millennials and Boomers Can Learn from Gen X Managers." Fast Company. May 22, 2018. https://www.fastcompany.com/40568780/this-is-what-millennials-and-boomers-can-learn-from-gen-x-mangers

4 Napach, Bernice. "Gen Xers Are Falling Behind Financially."

15 Craver, Jack. "Gen X: The 'Forgotten Generation' Gets Overlooked for Workplace Promotions." Benefits Pro. July 31, 2019. https://www.benefitspro.com/2019/07/31/gen-x-the-forgotten-generation-gets-overlooked-for-workplace-promotions/

[16] Neal, Stephanie. "Are Companies About to Have a Gen X Retention Problem?"

[17] John Hancock Retirement Plan Services. "Gen X Needs Help with Financial Wellness."

[18] MetLife. "Navigating Together: Supporting Employee Well-Being in Uncertain Times." 2020. https://www.metlife.com/employee-benefit-trends/ebts2020-holistic-well-being-drives-workforce-success/

[19] Kuehner-Hebert, Katie. "What Benefits Matter Most to Gen Xers?" Benefits Pro. January 10, 2018. https://www.benefitspro.com/2018/01/10/what-benefits-matter-most-to-gen-xers/

[20] Kuehner-Hebert, Katie. "What Benefits Matter Most to Gen Xers?"

[21] John Hancock Retirement Plan Services. "Gen X Needs Help with Financial Wellness."

[22] Craver, Jack. "Gen X: The 'Forgotten Generation' Gets Overlooked."

[23] Cross, James. "Boardroom Briefing: Engaging a New Generation of Investors." Franklin Templeton. nd. https://www.franklintempleton.com/investor/article?contentPath=html/ftthinks/en-us-retail/boardroom-briefing-engaging-a-new-generation-of-investors.html

[24] MetLife. Demographic Shifts, Employee Expectations Are Redefining the Workplace." April 3, 2017. https://www.metlife.com/about-us/newsroom/2017/april/demographic-shifts-employee-expectations-are-redefining-the-workplace/

[25] Neal, Stephanie. "Are Companies About to Have a Gen X Retention Problem?"

[26] Robison, Jennifer. "Why Millennials Are Job Hopping." Gallup. October 28, 2019. https://www.gallup.com/workplace/267743/why-millennials-job-hopping.aspx

[27] Lincoln Financial Group. "Millennials and Workplace Benefits: What Really Matters." nd. https://lincoln-financial.lfg.com/ LP=141/BetsySorensenLQQLDA?utm_source=rps_eloqua&utm_ medium=lp&utm_content=RPS20-CP-MILMS-WPG001_1&elqTrackId= f58e4091cd524f448b2571dbc33e83dd&elq=ebb001dc6cd94d449f55509fc 6cd3a26&elqaid=142&elqat=2&elqCampaignId=

[28] Hoffower, Hillary. "Meet the Average American Millennial, Who Has an $8,000 Net Worth, Is Delaying Life Milestones Due to Student-Loan Debt, and Still Relies on Parents for Money. Business Insider. February 27, 2020. https://www.businessinsider.com/average-american-millennial-net-worth- student-loan-debt-savings-habits-2019-6#and-the-typical-millennial-has- less-than-5000-in-their-savings-account-3

[29] Cheng, Marguerita. "8 Characteristics of Millennials that Support Sustainable Development." *Forbes.* June 19, 2019. https://www.forbes.com/ sites/margueritacheng/2019/06/19/8-characteristics-of-millennials-that- support-sustainable-development-goals-sdgs/?sh=6d89a6d829b7

[30] Cheng, Marguerita. "8 Characteristics of Millennials."

[31] Cussen, Mark P. "Money Habits of Millennials." Investopedia. March 21, 2020. https://www.investopedia.com/articles/personal-finance/021914/ money-habits-millennials.asp

[32] Cheng, Marguerita. "8 Characteristics of Millennials."

[33] Lincoln Financial Group. "Millennials and Workplace Benefits."

[34] Leonhardt, Megan. "Millennials Have an Average of $28,000 in Debt— And the Biggest Source Isn't Student Loans. CNBC. September 18, 2019. https://www.cnbc.com/2019/09/18/student-loans-are-not-the-no-1-source- of-millennial-debt.html

[35] Leonhardt, Megan. "Nearly 1 in 4 Millennials Report Having $100,000 or More in Savings." CNBC. January 30, 2020. https://www.cnbc. com/2020/01/30/nearly-1-in-4-millennials-report-having-100000- or-more-in-savings.html#:~:text=About%20three%20out%20of%20 four,Boomer%20parents%20(age%2033)

36 Leonhardt, Megan. "Nearly 1 in 4 Millennials Report Having $100,000 or More."

37 Randstad. "5 Common Myths about Millennials in the Workplace Debunked." June 4, 2020. https://www.randstad.com/workforce-insights/employer-branding/5-common-myths-about-millennials-workplace-debunked/

38 Costanza, David P.; Badger, Jessica M.; Fraser, Rebecca L.; Severt, Jamie B., and Gade, Paul A. "Generational Differences in Work-Related Attitudes: A Meta-Analysis." *Journal of Business and Psychology*. SpringerLink. March 11, 2012. https://link.springer.com/article/10.1007/s10869-012-9259-4

Chapter 7

1 Alpkunt, Berkay. "History of Steam Power: The Steam Engine Timeline." Evren Atlasi. February 28, 2020. https://evrenatlasi.com/en/2020/02/history-of-steam-power-the-steam-engine-timeline/

2 Bank of America. "2019 Workplace Benefits Report." nd. https://www.benefitplans.baml.com/publish/content/application/pdf/GWMOL/2019WorkplaceBenefitsReport.pdf

3 Business Roundtable. "Leadership in Action: Our Commitment to our Employees and Communities." nd. https://opportunity.businessroundtable.org/ourcommitment/

4 Corporate Leadership Center. "The Future of Work: Understanding the Changing Employer/Employee Relationship." July 2019. https://corporateleadership.org/understanding-the-changing-employer-employee-relationship/

Chapter 8

Alban, Kris. "How to Create Employee Financial Wellness Programs that Lead to Lasting Behavior Change." Benefits Pro. May 13, 2019. https://www.benefitspro.com/2019/05/13/how-to-create-employee-financial-wellness-programs-that-lead-to-lasting-behavior-change/

[2] Johndrow, Stefanie and Wiker, Noelle. "Carnegie Mellon Launches First Behavioral Economics Ph.D. Program." Carnegie Mellon University. December 20, 2017. https://www.cmu.edu/dietrich/news/news-stories/2017/december/phd-behavioral-economics.html

[3] Gino, Francesca. "The Rise of Behavioral Economics and Its Influence on Organizations." Harvard Business Review. October 10, 2017. https://hbr.org/2017/10/the-rise-of-behavioral-economics-and-its-influence-on-organizations

[4] Malmendier, Ulrike and Taylor, Timothy. "On the Verges of Overconfidence." *Journal of Economic Perspectives*. Fall 2015. https://eml.berkeley.edu/~ulrike/Papers/JEP_On_the_Verges.pdf

[5] Thaler, Richard H. and Sunstein, Cass R. (2009). *Nudge*. New York: Penguin Random House. https://www.penguinrandomhouse.com/books/304634/nudge-by-richard-h-thaler-and-cass-r-sunstein/

Chapter 9

Chandler, Simon. "Coronavirus Drives 72% Rise in Use of Fintech Apps." *Forbes*. March 30, 2020. https://www.forbes.com/sites/simonchandler/2020/03/30/coronavirus-drives-72-rise-in-use-of-fintech-apps/?sh=1d86052c66ed

[2] Peters, Adele. "Most Millennials Would Take a Pay Cut to Work at an Environmentally Sustainable Company." *Fast Company*. February 14, 2019. https://www.fastcompany.com/90306556/most-millennials-would-take-a-pay-cut-to-work-at-a-sustainable-company

Chapter 10

"Fintech Startups Raised $8.8bn in H1 2020, a 20% Drop Year-on-Year." nd. The Financial. https://www.finchannel.com/business/financial-markets-and-stocks/78198-fintech-startups-raised-8-8bn-in-h1-2020-a-20-drop-year-on-year#:~:text=The%20CrunchBase%20data%20revealed%20t-hat,the%20first%20quarter%20of%202019.

[2] Ghosh, Iman. "Visualizing the Current Landscape of the Fintech Industry." Visual Capitalist. January 28, 2020. https://www.visualcapitalist.com/current-fintech-industry/

[3] Barrett, Sam. "How Fintech Is Disrupting Workplace Health and Wellbeing." Corporate Adviser. September 17, 2019. https://corporate-adviser.com/how-fintech-is-disrupting-workplace-health-and-wellbeing/

[4] Wooldridge, Scott. "Using Big Data to Design Better Health Care Plans." Benefits Pro. March 7, 2018. https://www.benefitspro.com/2018/03/07/using-big-data-to-design-better-health-care-plans/

[5] Dash, Cindy. "How Companies Are Using Tech to Boost their Employees' Financial Wellness and Loyalty." Benefits Pro. March 4, 2020. https://www.benefitspro.com/2020/03/04/how-companies-are-using-tech-to-boost-their-employees-financial-wellness-and-loyalty/

[6] Corporate Wellness Magazine. "How to Make Big Data Work for Your Wellness Program." nd. https://www.corporatewellnessmagazine.com/article/big-data-work-wellness-program

Chapter 11

[1] "Financial Wellness Census: The Interplay Between Health and Financial Wellness Benefits and How It Impacts Employees." 2019. Prudential.

INDEX

ABOUT THE AUTHOR

Daniel Bryant is an author, adjunct lecturer, entrepreneur, philanthropist, and Iron Man. The first member of his family born in the United States, Daniel was a student athlete at Dartmouth College, where he received a BA in Government and Spanish and played shortstop on the baseball team. Subsequently, he received his MBA from the Kellogg School of Management at Northwestern University.

After a successful career in investment banking and private equity, Daniel cofounded Sheridan Road Financial, which ultimately grew to become the number-three-ranked institutional investment consulting company in the country, according to *Barron's* and *The Wall Street Journal*. After fifteen years as CEO of Sheridan Road, the company was sold to Hub International, the fourth largest insurance brokerage firm in the country.

Daniel has consulted with thousands of companies and been a thought leader around financial wellness and financial technology to help drive better health, financial, and life outcomes for individuals.

Daniel is Chairman of The Sheridan Road Charitable Foundation, which helps to improve the outcomes for those in under-resourced communities and in underperforming urban school systems. Daniel is an active board member with YPO Chicago Metro, The School of the Art Institute of Chicago, Hopkins Center, and Oz Arts. He is also a member of the Commercial Club of Chicago, Economic Club of Chicago, as well as the Chicago Club, and Standard Club of Nashville.

Daniel lives in Chicago and Nashville with his two daughters, Ainsley and Lily.

BE THE EMPLOYER OF CHOICE

Build a Business that Thrives in the Decade Ahead and Beyond

Daniel Bryant is available for:

- Consultancy
- Appearances
- Speaking Engagements

For more information, contact:
daniel@financialwellnessmandate.com